A Taste of Norwegian Nature
- along a waterway

Arne Brimi and Bengt Wilson

A Taste of Norwegian Nature
- along a waterway

Universitetsforlaget
Scandinavian University Press

Questions regarding this book can be addressed to:

UNIVERSITETSFORLAGET AS
Postboks 2959 Tøyen
N - 0608 Tøyen
Norway

Photographs: Bengt Wilson
Layout: Arne Vetlli'n and Dole Norum
Typesetting: Arne Vetlli'n
Cover Photograph: Bengt Wilson
Cover Layout: Dole Norum
Repro and Printing: Tangen Grafiske Senter AS, Drammen, 1993
Binding: Refsum Bokbinderi AS, Oslo
Translation and Adaptation: Melody Favish

Title page motif is a bronze age stone carving.
Source: Dairy Products: A century of Norwegian milk producers, 1981

This book is one of the series of quality books included in the
Cultural programme of the XVII Olympic Winter Games at
Lillehammer in 1994. It has been published in collaboration with
De norske Bokklubbene AS.

Contents

A Taste of Norwegian Nature - along a waterway

Along a waterway - water is the source of life. Even in the most desolate of landscapes, wherever there is water, there is greenery.

Along a waterway - in a wide perspective - it is the water which determines the culture around it. When early man first settled down from his nomadic existence, he did it with a source of water at hand. It is not without reason that great cities often are along rivers. London has the Thames, Paris the Seine, New Orleans the Mississippi, and Trondheim the Nidar. Without these rivers, the cities would have been established elsewhere.

Along a waterway is an unusual title for a cookbook, but there is some logic to it.

Where I live, food has always been connected with water. In the Otta valley, agriculture is dependent upon irrigation for crops.

In certain parts of my home region, the annual precipitation can be compared with that of the Sahara desert. For that reason, water is the limiting factor for farming. Through hundreds of year, the people of our area have learned to make the best use of the sources they have. They dammed mountain ponds to tap as needed. They dug canals from deep in the mountains down to the farms, where it ran onto or was sprayed over fields and meadows. Watering was so important that a tool which was used for spraying appeared on a local banner as early as the Middle Ages. That banner hangs in Lom church today.

With enough water, the farms in the Otta valley were reasonably secure. In fact, local farms produced enough grain to supply other districts, until the building of the railroad made cheaper English grain accessible, and the Otta farmers no longer could compete.

The waterway - whether it flows in a stream or through the tap - is the basis for all life. In addition, it is an important element of the landscape and it is part of the culture as well.

The waterway - river, sea, ocean. All have a timeless quality. Every one of us has a place along a waterway for a time. It is our responsibility to take care of it and the culture around it, so that others also can enjoy it later.

In the kitchen, clean water is a necessity. Those who prepare food daily know just how important it is for good results. Clean water is important in the production of food, absolutely necessary for maintaining high standards. Water is the basis of all life. For that reason, it is troubling that water is so easy to pollute, that this aspect of our civilization can be a threat to future civilizations.

Clean water is the basic departure point for a good kitchen. The running mountain stream should be a symbol of our desire to preserve all that nature is for us. The old waterway, which saved the harvest for farmers and animals alike, is a reminder of all their hard work, and it can remind us of our responsibility to preserve our cultural heritage.

Welcome to a wandering through Nature's Kitchen

Lom, August, 1993

Arne Brimi

"Mom's Meat Cakes"

Food is culture – not just in Norway, but around the world. Gathering around a table for a meal is possibly the most important cultural element in all societies. For that reason, the roots of our culture are important. My own cultural background is firmly rooted in the area where I grew up, especially in the meals I ate at home with my mother. The food served to me as a child is my departure point for flavors, and tradition determines the ingredients. All this is taken into consideration when I discuss food and its preparation. This is one of the most important gifts of my upbringing, especially now that I have chosen to be a chef.

Many aspects about meals with my mother are special. I feel the most important part is the love which she has, both for those who enjoy the food and for the raw materials, along with her meticulousness, which has been handed down through generations. She grew up on a small farm, at Husehaugen, where I live now. Farming at Husehaugen has always been based on the principle of self-sufficiency. She learned to use every resource available, both within and beyond the fence. She worked in mountain hotels until she settled down with her family, and then she passed on the traditions which she had learned in the kitchens at home and at work.

I am fortunate to be able to enjoy a meal with my mother frequently. The menu is predictable, but that is a form of security. It's that way for me too, with my guests. I feel that it is important that my guests recognize something or other in my menus and dishes. I am not always sure that they knows what it is, but it is something which they identify, and that makes them feel secure.

I have selected a number of dishes from my mother's kitchen. These are special for her and special for me – good traditional food, with roots and a heritage, food which we really like.

That is the best thing I know.

Lamb and Cabbage Stew

Few Norwegian dishes are better known or more popular than lamb and cabbage stew. It's a favorite dish for many, and most agree with me that it tastes even better the day after it's made.

A meal I'll always remember included reheated lamb and cabbage stew. One August evening, Unni and I arrived, wet and cold, at Nørstedalssæter. We were starved, and we were the only guests. But there was lamb and cabbage stew. The hostess set a table before the fireplace, and the rewarmed stew was placed before us. There's an old saying that hunger is the best cook, but I must say that our hostess at Nørstedalssæter made the stew taste just like my mother's.

According to Henry Notaker, a Norwegian writer, lamb and cabbage stew is not such an old dish. And if he says that, it must be true, for few have studied our food culture more than Henry. He says that cabbage has been used in dishes prepared much like lamb and cabbage stew, but that particular combination is first mentioned in the early part of the last century. By the end of the century, it was already very popular. It is still common to use other types of meat, especially reindeer and hare, in this dish.

This is the way I make lamb and cabbage stew today.

1 kg (2 1/4 pounds) lamb or mutton shoulder, neck or breast
1/2 kg (1 pound) cabbage
4 teaspoons black peppercorns
1 tablespoon salt
5 dl (2 cups) boiling water or stock

Cut the meat into serving pieces, removing some of the fat. Clean the cabbage and cut into wedges. Layer the meat, fat side down, and the cabbage in a large pot, sprinkling each layer with peppercorns and salt. The top layer should be cabbage.

Pour over the liquid to reach about 5-6 cm (2") over the top layer of cabbage. Bring to a boil, cover and simmer over low heat until the meat is tender, about 90 minutes. Shake the pot several times during cooking, so that the meat doesn't stick to the bottom. Do not stir, or the cabbage will fall apart. Serve with boiled potatoes and flatbread. Serves 4-6.

Liver in Cream Sauce

In the olden days, nothing was wasted, and organ meats and blood were especially prized. I like liver best, especially liver in cream sauce, which appeared often on our table.

Beef and pork liver are good, but the best and most festive is calf's liver.

600 g (1 1/3 pounds) liver
3 tablespoons flour
salt and freshly ground white pepper
2 tablespoons butter
2-3 dl (1 cup) whipping cream

Remove large veins and membrane from the liver. Cut into 1 cm (3/16") slices. Dip in flour seasoned with salt and pepper. Sauté in butter over medium heat 7-8 minutes, turning often. Add the cream and simmer 2-3 minutes.

Transfer the liver to a serving platter, then reduce the cream sauce over high heat a few minutes more. Nap the liver with the sauce. Serve with boiled potatoes and lingonberry compote. Serves 4.

Meat Cakes, Brown Gravy and Creamed Cabbage

Years ago, the slaughtering season meant intense activity, usually with the help of friends and relatives. Good conversation punctuated with laughter helped the hard work go faster.

Meat cakes, one of our truly authentic national dishes, has withstood a lot of abuse over the past years. Originally they were made from ground beef, while sausage patties were made from ground pork. Today, it is quite common to make meat cakes from a mixture of ground beef and pork. This recipe makes meat cakes just the way I like them.

1 kg (2 1/4 pounds) boneless
    beef - chuck or round
2 teaspoons salt
1 teaspoon freshly ground white pepper
1/2 teaspoon ground ginger
2 tablespoons potato starch
5 dl (2 cups) milk or water
butter

1 liter (quart) beef stock

Cut the meat into chunks and grind 3-4 times. Add seasonings and starch, mixing well. Gradually add the liquid. Make oval cakes, about 60 g (2 ounces) each. Brown in butter on both sides.

Bring the stock to a simmer, then add the meat cakes. Simmer 10-15 minutes. Remove from the stock, then cool. Serves 4-6.

Some prefer to use other seasonings, especially allspice. An egg can be added to bind, if desired.

My favorite meat cakes are those canned in big jars by my mother.

Creamed Cabbage

about 500 g (1 pound) cabbage
water
2 teaspoons salt

Sauce

2 tablespoons butter or margarine
4 tablespoons (1/4 cup) flour
4 dl (1 2/3 cups) milk
1/4 teaspoon nutmeg
salt

Brown Gravy

2 1/2 tablespoons butter

2 1/2 tablespoons flour
5 dl (2 cups) boiling pan juices or stock
salt and pcpper
cream

Clean the cabbage and cut into 1 1/2 cm (3/4")
cubes. Cook 25-30 minutes in lightly salted
water. Drain. Melt the butter in a saucepan, then
stir in the flour. Gradually, whisk in the milk
and bring to a boil, stirring constantly. Simmer
8-10 minutes. Add the drained, cooked cabbage,
bring to a boil, then season with salt and nutmeg. Brown the butter and flour in a cast iron
pan over low heat, stirring constantly. Gradually
whisk in the boiling liquid, stirring until
smooth. Simmer 10-15 minutes. Season with
salt, pepper and, if desired, a little cream.

11

Boiled Beef and Soup

Another favorite dish is boiled meat, prepared the traditional way, preferably with several kinds of meat in the pot. This is good food for any occasion, as well as a national dish in many countries.

As a cook, I do not feel that a dinner has to be formal to be a success. Set a pot of boiled beef in front of anyone, and I guarantee that the dinner will be a success. Just imagine guests walking into your home and being greeted by the wonderful aroma!

Good luck.

1 1/2 kg (3 pounds) beef chuck, blade or
   arm roast
marrow bones (if using boneless meat)
water
4 teaspoons salt
8-10 white peppercorns
1 bay leaf
2 teaspoons thyme
parsley
4 carrots, in chunks
1 leek, in chunks
1/4 cabbage, in small wedges
1/2 small rutabaga, in chunks

Arrange the meat and bones in a large pot. Add water to cover. Add salt and slowly bring to a boil. Skim well.

Add seasonings, cover and simmer 90 minutes. Add vegetables and simmer until tender, 20-30 minutes. Remove the meat from the pot, slice and serve with the vegetables. Strain the soup, then skim off as much fat as possible. The soup can be served clear or with vegetables.

If marrow bones have been cooked with the soup, they should be served alongside. It might be necessary to wrap them in cheesecloth before cooking, to keep the marrow from falling out. Serves 4.

Fried Pollack with Onions

The selection of saltwater fish in an inland district is self-limiting, and for many years, there just wasn't much good fish available. Once the permanent road over the Stryn mountains was opened at the end of the 1970's, it became easier to transport fish from the west coast.

Until that time, we used mostly freshwater fish, such as grayling and trout. With Vågå lake just outside my door, I have spent many summer hours fishing, and if I feel like a walk in the mountains, I can go and fish trout.

Salt herring with beets, onions and potatoes, and maybe some other side dishes, are considered a delicacy today. It wasn't that long ago that salt herring was considered poor man's food. I have always liked to eat salt herring, but I don't like to clean them. They appeared often on our dinner table.

Fried pollack was another enjoyable dish. Fried pollack with onions is a traditional meal, which, unfortunately, seldom appears on restaurant menus.

600 g (1 1/3 pounds) skinless and boneless pollack fillets
2 tablespoons flour
salt and white pepper
3-4 onions, sliced
clarified butter

Cut the fillets into serving pieces. Dip in flour seasoned with salt and pepper. Sauté the onions in butter until soft but not brown. Remove from the pan and keep warm. Fry the fish until golden brown over medium heat, turning often. They should take 7-8 minutes. Serve with the onions, browned butter and cole slaw. Serves 4.

Fried Bread with Gudbrandsdal Cheese and Milk

My mother used to serve this dish for a simple dinner - maybe to use up old bread, or just to take it easy in the kitchen.

2 tablespoons butter
6 slices bread
3 dl (1/4 cups) milk
8-10 slices Gudbrandsdal cheese (Ski Queen)
4 teaspoons sugar

Heat the butter in a frying pan. Fry the bread on both sides. Add the milk. Top the bread with the cheese and cover. Cook 3-4 minutes, until the cheese melts slightly. Sprinkle with sugar and serve. Serves 4.

This dish also tastes good with a sprinkling of ground cloves and a handful of blueberries in the pan.

Dessert

Dessert is not an longstanding tradition in most homes. When I was a child, we hardly ever had dessert, at most once or twice a week. But then we appreciated it all the more.

Something to serve with coffee, however, was important. There always had to be homemade baked goods in the house, in case anyone dropped in for a visit, and my mother is a better baker than dessert maker. That is probably true for many other housewives.

We often have sweet dishes served as part of a meal. These include berry soup with barley, prune soup, barley cooked in milk and served with cinnamon sugar, and we mustn't forget fresh rhubarb soup, served warm or cold.

Summer and fall are the best times for dessert. Dessert season begins with rhubarb, then later in the summer come wild strawberries, and after that both wild and domesticated berries, good times for anyone with a sweet tooth.

I have chosen two of my favorite desserts.

Red Porridge

Early autumn is jam and juice making time. We always have enough fruit and berries in our garden and in the nearby woods, so we never have to buy jam or juice. This porridge is winter food with the flavor of summer.

    6 dl (2 1/2 cups) red currant, strawberry
      or raspberry juice concentrate
    6 dl (2 1/2 cups) water
    6 tablespoons potato starch (or cornstarch)
    2 teaspoons sugar

Combine juice concentrate, water and potato starch in a saucepan. Bring to a boil, stirring constantly, then remove from the heat immediately. Pour into a serving bowl. Sprinkle with sugar and let cool. Serve lukewarm or cold with milk or half and half. Serves 4.

Red Currants with Vanilla Sauce

Vanilla Sauce

    2 eggs
    3 tablespoons sugar
    1 tablespoon potato starch (or cornstarch)
    8 dl (3 1/3 cups) milk
    2 tablespoons vanilla sugar
      (or 1 tablespoon vanilla extract)
    4 tablespoons (1/4 cup) whipping cream

Red Currant Compote

    400 g (14 ounces) ripe, stemmed red currants
    100 g (3 1/2 ounces, 1 1/4 dl, 1/2 cup) sugar

There are many recipes for vanilla sauce, but my mother's is easy to make and tastes good.

Whisk together eggs, sugar, potato starch and a few spoonfuls of milk in a saucepan. Whisk in the remaining milk. Cook over low heat until thick, whisking constantly. Stir in the vanilla and chill. Just before serving, whip the cream and fold into the sauce.

Place the currants and the sugar in a food processor and pulse several times, until the mixture is pink and foamy. Serves 4.

Dairy Life

Gudbrandsdal and Valdres have the richest dairy traditions in the country. High season on mountain dairies usually started in late June. Long ago, many farms had two dairy barns, one close to the farm and another in the mountains.

Grazing in the mountains produced the best butter and cheese. Mountain dairies are an old tradition in Norway. Many feel that they came about because the number of farms increased as population grew, and with that came a corresponding increase in stock. New grazing areas were needed, and that meant climbing higher and higher up the mountainsides.

Eventually, they were so high up in the mountains that it was necessary to build a cabin there for both milkmaids and cows. That way, the milk could be processed on the spot.

Hygiene always has been important at these mountain dairies in Gudbrandsdal. Everything used in the processing of milk was washed and scrubbed daily – not just the tools, but the entire building, with tables and benches. That was part of the milkmaid's job.

The attention paid to cleanliness made the products produced in the mountain farms of Gudbrandsdal more desirable.

Even though the mountain farm season is only three months, the buildings are used almost year-round. In the Vågå region, farmers used to go up the mountain in the fall and stay there until the hay, leaves and moss which had been collected on the mountain were used up. They did that instead of making many trips with hay and moss on unpaved paths. It was tough work, but I think people enjoyed themselves.

Milkmaids usually spent many summers at the same mountain farm, and a good milkmaid was a treasure. When she came home in the fall, a party was held in her honor.

Otherwise, the mountain farms were used for fall fishing and winter hunting. Especially during the late winter, when there was not much

work to do on the farm, many went up the mountains to hunt and trap ptarmigan. Then it was handy to have a cabin there.

I have an aunt who has been a milkmaid for many years. The job is much easier now, but both Embjørg and many others like to preserve the old traditions. In fact, there's a growing interest in that.

From the time I learned to walk, it was a part of our summer routine to visit Aunt Embjørg. I understood early on just how special life at a mountain farm was. Many aspects of life there belonged to a lifestyle completely foreign to most. The milkmaids got together, they led the cows to the grassy areas, and then they led them home for the night. Maybe a suitor visited on Saturday evening. On weekends, cityfolk climbed up to these cabins for a visit, to pick cloudberries and to eat good dairy meals. They breathed in the hot smells of the barn, drank the creamy milk and enjoyed all the interesting stories about elves, trolls and witches told while sitting by the fire. I've never seen an elf, but I know that they exist.

Dairy Dishes

It wasn't easy to make a meal at a mountain dairy because of the limited cooking possibilities. And, there were so many everyday chores that there was little time to prepare food. Most of the time, one-dish meals were the norm.

Mountain dairies and sour cream go together. Even though the Norwegian dairies make good sour cream, there's nothing like tasting sour cream made on the spot at a mountain dairy.

I don't remember Aunt Embjørg ever being particularly generous with cloudberries (orange berries, which look like raspberries, but which taste more like a combination of peaches, mangoes and passion fruit). We didn't get to pick much, either, because she didn't want to reveal where they were. Maybe she didn't find too many of them, either.

But there was a little, and they were served with sour cream and waffles as dinner or with coffee, usually on weekends. Dairy dishes can be served anywhere, on just about any occasion. Just imagine a plate of sour cream with a generous spoonful of berries and hot, crispy dessert waffles alongside.

Sour Cream with Berries and Waffles

4 dl (1 2/3 cups) whipping cream
   or 35% fat sour cream
1 dl (1/3 cup) water
3 dl (1 2/3 cups) flour

Sour Cream with Berries

sour cream
cloudberries or other berries

Whip the cream or the sour cream. If using sour cream, it first becomes thin, then it peaks. Fold in the water and flour. Let the batter rest 30 minutes before cooking. Bake waffles until golden and crispy. Makes 10-12.

Spoon the sour cream into a bowl. Top with fresh berries and serve with crispy waffles.

Barley Cream Porridge

This porridge is traditional sour cream porridge stretched with barley, or sometimes rice. This made the most of what was available. Of course, it wasn't considered as fine as sour cream porridge.

Barley has been used from early times, but as rice began to be imported to Norway, it sometimes replaced barley. Rice was considered better, perhaps because of its white color. It gave this traditional dish an exotic touch.

3 dl (1 1/4 cups) whole barley
about 1 liter (quart) milk
2 liters (quarts) whipping cream
5 dl (2 cups) 35% fat sour cream
5 dl (2 cups) flour
1-2 dl (1/2 cup) boiling milk

Soak the barley overnight. Drain, then simmer in milk to a thick porridge, about 1 hour. Bring cream and sour cream to a boil and simmer 15 minutes. Sift over the flour, stirring well. It is important that the cream be boiling at all times. Simmer until the butterfat begins to leach out. Skim off the fat. Thin with boiling milk. Combine this cream porridge with the barley porridge and serve. Serves 12-14.

Because this porridge is not as heavy and filling as sour cream porridge, I like it better.

Note: It is essential to use natural 35% fat sour cream in this dish. It will not work with low fat sour cream or sour cream which contains gelatin or stabilizers.

Flatbread Soup and Dried Meats

Flatbread soup sounds strange, but it tastes good. There are probably other names for this summer dish. It tastes best at the mountain dairy farm, especially when served with a good air-dried ham.

Crumble homemade flatbread into a bowl. Top with buttermilk and maybe a spoonful of sour cream.

Ideally, the flatbread should be homemade. I usually say that there is only one kind of flatbread; homemade.

Bacon Pancake

400 g (14 ounces) streaky bacon or salt pork
  in one piece
3 eggs
8 dl (3 1/3 cups) milk
4 dl (1 2/3 cups) flour

Cut the bacon into 1/2 cm (1/5") slices. Dry fry until crisp. Drain off all but about 1 tablespoon of the fat. Whisk together eggs, milk and flour and pour over the bacon. Cover and cook over low heat 8-10 minutes. Serves 4.

This is a simple but hearty dish, which makes the most out of bacon and a few eggs.

Berry Pie

Life at the mountain dairy has changed considerably since the last war. It has already been many years since electricity was installed, even at Tesse, and that made just about everything easier.
Aunt Embjørg knew her way around a kitchen, thanks to her mother, Helen, my grandmother. She was known for her food.

Embjørg makes Grandmother's blueberry pie almost as good as Grandmother did. It can be served as a dessert or with a cup of coffee.

Pastry

4 dl (1 2/3 cups) flour
150 g (5 ounces, 2/3 cup) unsalted butter
1 teaspoon salt
3-4 tablespoons water
1 tablespoon sugar

Filling

1 liter (quart) fresh blueberries
3 tablespoons sugar
2 tablespoons flour

Preheat the oven to 180 °C (350 °F). Quickly combine the pastry ingredients in a food processor or with a pastry blender. Divide in two and roll out half to a thin sheet slightly larger than the pie plate. Place in the bottom. Sprinkle with sugar.

Sprinkle the berries over the crust. Sprinkle with sugar and flour. Brush the edges of the bottom crust with water. Roll out the remaining pastry and lay on top. Pinch top and bottom crust together. Prick the top crust with a fork, so that steam can escape. Bake 45 minutes. Serve with cream.

Fried Trout with Sour Cream Sauce

The thought of plump mountain trout awakens pleasant associations for most people. There's something special about the fish. In our area, local patriotism determines which lake has the best fish.

At Nordsætrene, where Embjørg is milkmaid, Tesse lake is just below the mountain dairy. Tesse fish are, of course, best. Maybe they are, too, at least no worse than any other fish. For a milkmaid who doesn't fish, even with a lake nearby, it isn't always easy to make a weekend dinner.

One who does catch fish, Sigurd Biløygard, has a cabin right by Tesse and fishes all summer. Many know Sigurd, so whoever has the best sour cream can trade it for fish for a good dinner. At any rate, fresh trout with sour cream sauce is a delicious dish, especially when served in a mountain cabin.

Clean the fish well, rinsing out all the blood along the backbone, then dry with paper towels. Scale the fish. Dredge in flour and fry in butter over medium heat, turning often. This should take 12-14 minutes.

When almost done, pour sour cream into the pan and sprinkle with chopped chives. Let bubble a few minutes, season with salt and serve with the fish and boiled almond potatoes.

Lillehammer Olympics '94

The 1994 Olympics are a big arrangement – an event, not just for the region around the Mjøsa lake and Gudbrandsdal, but for the country as a whole, and for many years in to the future. Just as the 1952 Olympics in Oslo were and are, the Lillehammer games will be even moreso. Everything that happens in our own lifetime seems closer, and for that reason, most of us will have a personal relationship with the games.

Sport, of course, and culture are very important to the games. I've always been interested in sport, and especially in culture. As far as I am concerned, food is the most important cultural entity we have. The district in which the 1994 games are being held is, in many ways, characteristic of our country. We can be proud of the diversity in our district, which includes mountains, plains, high-altitude fields and forests with the finest game imaginable. Our agriculture includes both livestock and crops. We have plants and herbs which provide endless variation when used with all the fine raw materials. And, in addition, we have our cultural heritage, which we take care to preserve.

The first Norwegians settled along the coast because it was easier to get food there. Nature is usually the decisive factor for settlement, even in Gudbrandsdal. There were animals and plants in the mountains and valleys, there was water, and there was soil for crops, for getting enough food was of the utmost concern, then as now. From the first settlements to today is a long story and a colossal development, but it still involves getting enough food. And we are still dependent upon nature to provide the right conditions.

It's like that all over the world, not just here. If we are to add anything to that foundation, we have to be familiar with our own historical development and to know what our past has given us. Norway has developed solid traditions fostered by individuality over hundreds of years, and we must continue in this same manner, so that we will retain this spirit in the future. We like to be thought of as solid and honest and with an identity. It's that way with food, too. We want to have quality, resources and possibilities in the future, and the best way to assure that is

to take care of them now – I think we can manage that.

The Olympic area is a typical inland district, but as far as food is concerned, it is still representative of the country as a whole, especially today, with easy access to fresh ingredients from the coast and from other regions of the country.

Clean, true and basic are important words, more important than ever. As a cook, I appreciate every possibility I get to live by these words, and at the same time know that they are true.

We have a kitchen with an identity and a cultural connection. It's more than a little handwork, bound together with considerable reflection. Nothing is good without a philosophy.

Olympic Food

Since September 15, 1988, when Lillehammer was named host of the 1994 Olympics, everyone in Norway, not just in Lillehammer and Gudbrandsdal, has regarded the Olympics as a great sporting and cultural event.

This has been an exciting time, with new ideas in every aspect of business. My role has been to create new dishes and serving possibilities based on the traditional production and use of Norwegian ingredients. Most represent my home district, but I also have included others. Food is more and more often used to underline our special traditions, not only food traditions, but just about everything else, too. The serving of food can be a bridge to understanding. Then the food should be exciting, and that we can manage. Above all, our basic ingredients come from an agriculture with high moral principles, and we have all reason to be proud of that.

I have been a member of the national culinary team, which, like all other national teams, competes in the "Culinary Olympics" every four years in Frankfurt. This competition also has official status as an Olympics. We have been abroad on many assignments, both on our own and representing Norway. One of our biggest projects was in Albertville, where we hosted the closing dinner for the 1992 Olympics.

In addition, I have personally been involved on many occasions in Lillehammer, where I have served both my food and my philosophy. I've served dinners, buffets and finger food. Let these dishes be my contribution to our discussion on how we should preserve our traditions for the future.

Dairy Products

It is only natural to begin with dairy products. They have been and still are the basis of nourishment. We have the oldest traditions in the development of dairy products and the perfection of the qualities which milk can give. The most important dairy product throughout our history has been butter. It was butter which made the Norwegian farmer keep livestock. It is not unreasonable to believe that keeping livestock may have begun as long as 6000 years ago. That shows how important a source of nourishment milk and milk products always have been. Butter has been used both as a measure of value and as a form of currency.

The development of the modern dairy as we know it today began in the 1800's. Livestock specialists and cheesemakers were brought in from Switzerland to teach Norwegian farmers more about keeping animals and making cheese, and training of "cheese girls" was established. They went around the country and taught people about the production of butter and cheese. Their importance can be understood, when one considers that the foreman on a dairy farm is called a "sveiser" or Swiss.

Gudbrandsdal valley is made up of hillside settlements. The farther north and west, the craggier the landscape. It is in these hilly areas that livestock and milk production have been the most important basis for the farming of cows and goats. The products the animals produced were a good source of income, and during the summer and fall, different products could be stored for use during the rest of the year. On big farms, with several generations of farmers and many hired hands, a big storehouse was needed. Many, though, were unable to store much of anything for the winter.

Self-sufficiency was the only way to survive, so most people tried to have a piece of land. The next goal was to be able to keep a cow. And one can imagine all the hard work to gather enough food for the cow to last the winter. Leaves and moss were collected, hay and grass was gathered.

Even so, nothing was left when spring came. We have heard stories of animals so weak that they had to be carried out of the barn to eat the first green shoots of grass in the spring.

In 1856, Norway and northern Europe's first cooperative dairy was started at Raudsjødalen with 40 members. This arrangement served as the basis for others, and eventually many cheese factories were built in the area. In 1900, there were 780, the highest number ever in Norway.

These mostly produced hard cheeses such as Swiss and Edam. Swiss cheese gets its name from all the Swiss who came here to teach us about cheesemaking. Eventually, the cheese factories began combining the production of butter with the making of lower fat cheeses. During the 1900's and the time between the wars, hard times came, which eventually led to a more centralized production, with less destructive competition among the smaller dairies. By 1930, the milk producers in the country joined together under a shelter organization.

Today, we know this organization as Norwegian Dairies, with Tine as its trade name. We know that Norwegian dairy products are especially good. Impeccable morals among producers with high standards, as well as sensible research and good quality control, have given Norwegian agriculture the most healthy cows in the world, the Norwegian red, known by the initials NRF.

All the above, plus animals grazing outside much of the year, means livestock with a good quality of life and consistent high quality raw materials.

Gudbrandsdal Cheese

Few things have been more important for the economy of Gudbrandsdal than Gudbrandsdal cheese. Just about everyone likes it and uses it. It has its place on most breakfast and lunch tables, and a few years ago, it was voted the most typical of all things Norwegian.

It was first made in Gudbrandsdal in 1863 by milkmaid Anne Hov. She worked with her father at the Solbrå mountain dairy at Valsæter on Fron mountain.

Sometimes the best new products are discovered by accident. But as I know the story, it appears that Anne Hov did a good bit of thinking before she started her experiment. She asked her father if she could make a new and better cheese. The cheese, which is firm, was made in an iron pot. She reduced the sweet whey with cream slowly, stirring constantly, so that the

cheese took on the color, consistency and the characteristic caramel taste which we know so well. Then it was poured into molds and allowed to harden.

Nothing else happened with Gudbrandsdal cheese until many years later. Then Anne Hov was married to Tor Hov, and they had moved to a farm in Nord-Fron called Rusthage. At that time, they delivered milk to the cheese factory at Ruste, and milk prices were very low. Worst of all was the long journey to the cheese factory with the milk.

She tells the story that early one morning, when the milk was already on the sled ready to be driven to the cheese factory, the horse became frightened and jumped, tipping out all the milk cans, spilling it everywhere. She became really angry, and thought about that cheese she used to make up in the mountains. She decided that it had to be possible to process the milk at home instead of sending it to the cheese factory. When she tried to make the cheese again, she added a little goat milk. The cheese was so good that a merchant in the area, Ole Kongsli, offered to sell as much as she could produce. He had contacts in the city, too, and eventually, more and more shipments of cheese were sent to the city.

The importance of Gudbrandsdal cheese was first realized in the 1870's. During that time, loads of grain were driven over the mountains – right after the middle of the century, about 1000 horses a year pulled grain on the road. Eventually, cheaper grain from other countries came onto the market. The Østerdal railroad came, and grain from Gudbrandsdal no longer could compete. That led to an economic crisis, which led to an even greater emphasis placed on livestock, and the production of butter, cheese and meat replaced grain.

That was when Gudbrandsdal cheese really saved the valley. Even though people then were critical of new things, many began to produce and sell the cheese. At one time, the price of the cheese was the same as for butter. But to make butter, much more milk is needed than for cheese.

Much loved children have many names. Here in Gudbrandsdal, we call the cheese "red cheese" because of its color. In other places, especially in the eastern regions of the country, it is called "goat cheese" even though there is only a small amount of goat milk in it. And in the rest of the country, there are probably other names.

But originally it is from Valsæter on Fron mountain, born in the year 1863, and in its 130th year, it has gotten a new name – the Olympic cheese.

We have a long and worthy tradition in our use of this cheese, and not just on the table. It is also popular to put a few slices of Gudbrandsdal cheese in a good sauce, especially for game.

There are many other ways to use the cheese. Since Gudbrandsdal cheese has such a central position in our economy, it is natural to begin with a few dishes using our national cheese.

Red Cheese Cream on Flatbread

100 g (4 ounces) Gudbrandsdal cheese
  (Ski Queen)
50 g (2 ounces, 1 dl, 1/3 cup)
  raw lingonberries
100 g (4 ounces, 1/2 cup) sour cream
flatbread or thin, unsalted wheat
  or rye crackers

Coarsely grate the cheese. Combine with lingonberries and sour cream. Serve on flatbread or crackers as finger food or as a dip.

Salad with Gudbrandsdal Cheese Croutons

Vinaigrette Dressing

1 tablespoon white or red wine vinegar
1 teaspoon salt
freshly ground white pepper
4 tablespoons (1/4 cup) oil

Salad

1 head lettuce
4 slices bread
1 tablespoon butter
8 slices Gusbrandsdal cheese (Ski Queen)
2 teaspoons chopped fresh thyme

Make the dressing first. Combine vinegar, salt and pepper, then whisk in the oil. Add fresh herbs, if desired.

Clean the lettuce and combine with the dressing. Arrange on individual dishes. Remove the crusts and cut the bread into 1 cm (3/16") cubes. Sauté in butter. When they begin to brown, add cheese and thyme. Cook until the pan is dry and the croutons are crisp. Sprinkle over the salad and serve either as an appetizer or as a light meal. Serves 4.

Gudbrandsdal Cheese and Aquavit-Marinated Lingonberries

The three main ingredients in this dish are very special and very Norwegian.

100 g (4 ounces, 2 1/2 dl,1 cup) raw
  lingonberries
50 g (2 ounces, 1 dl, 1/3 cup) unrefined or
  Demerara sugar
2 dl (3/4 cup) aquavit
100 g (4 ounces) grated Gudbrandsdal cheese
  (Ski Queen)

Marinate the berries with the sugar and aquavit 1 hour. With an electric mixer, beat until foamy, then gradually add the cheese. Spoon into egg cups or small bowls and freeze. Serve as a palate refreshener between fish and meat courses or as a small dessert.

Pear Tart with Brown Goat Cheese or Gudbrandsdal Cheese

Brown goat cheese, called "Ekte Geitost" in Norwegian, is made from 100% goat milk, while Gudbrandsdal cheese, exported as Ski Queen, is made from a blend of goat and cow milk. The former has a stronger flavor.

Pastry

200 g (7 ounces, 3 dl, 1 1/4 cups) flour
125 g (4 ounces, 1/2 cup) butter
75 g (3 ounces, scant 1 dl, 1/3 cup) sugar
1 egg white

Filling

3 firm pears
4 dl (1 2/3 cups) milk
200 g (7 ounces) brown goat cheese or Gudbrandsdal (Ski Queen) cheese
2 tablespoons honey
3-4 eggs

Quickly combine the pastry ingredients in a food processor or with a pastry blender. Gather into a ball, cover with plastic wrap and chill at least an hour. Roll out to a thin sheet and place in the bottom and up the sides of a 24 cm (10") springform.

Preheat the oven to 175 °C (350 °F). Peel, halve and core the pears. Arrange on the pastry. Bring milk, cheese and honey to a boil. Stir until the cheese is completely melted. Beat the eggs and gradually add the hot milk. Pour over the pears. Bake 40 minutes. Serve warm.

Lingonberries can be substituted for pears, but they need more honey or sugar.

Pultost and Gamalost

You either love or hate these two cheeses. *Pultost* is a rather sour curd cheese flavored with caraway. It is light golden in color and smells fermented. *Gamalost* is a medium brown, low fat, crumbly cheese which has a strong, almost ammonia odor.

Those of us who like strong cheeses know that they must be ripe to be good. *Gamalost* can't have a light center, and the best pultost should be so ripe that it is spreadable.

We aren't the only ones who like strong cheeses. Other countries have their own pungent varieties. It is important to continue producing these cheeses and to find new ways to serve them.

Warm Gamalost with Pears Poached with Black Currants

There is no substitute for *gamalost*.

4 teaspoons butter
4 slices gamalost, about 3-4 mm thick
chopped fresh (or crushed dry) thyme
pears poached with black currants
   (see recipe, page 128)

Preheat the oven to 150 °C (300 °F). Place a spoonful of butter on each cheese slice and sprinkle with thyme. Arrange on a cookie sheet and bake until the butter has melted into the cheese. Place the pears on individual dishes and top with the warm cheese. The cheese also tastes good with mixed berry yogurt or sour cream with lingonberry compote. Serves 4.

Strawberries au Gratin with Strawberry Purée and Vanilla Ice Cream

Hot and cold are always good together in a dessert. Here is a good recipe for homemade ice cream.

Vanilla Parfait (ice cream)

  8 egg yolks
  150 g (5 ounces, 1 1/2 dl, scant 2/3 cup) sugar
  2 teaspoons vanilla sugar
    (or 1 teaspoon vanilla extract)
  5 dl (2 cups) whipping cream

Strawberry Purée

  1 1/2 baskets (750 g, 1 2/3 pounds)
    strawberries or other berries
  1 tablespoon confectioner's sugar
  juice of 1/2 lemon
  1 1/2 dl (2/3 cup) whipping cream
  1 tablespoon chopped nuts

Beat the egg yolks with the sugar and vanilla until light and lemon-colored, about 5 minutes. Whip the cream and fold into the egg yolk mixture. Freeze in an ice cream machine or in a mold.

Purée 1/2 basket of berries with confectioner's sugar and lemon juice in a blender. Sieve. Transfer to an ovenproof dish. Preheat the grill. Slice the remaining berries and arrange them in the dish. Whip the cream and spread over the berries. Sprinkle with nuts. Grill until the cream is melted and golden. Serve with ice cream. Serves 8-10.

Salad with Glazed Gamalost

There is no substitute for *gamalost.*

Glaze

  1 dl (1/2 cup) unrefined or Demerara sugar
  1 dl (1/2 cup) cider vinegar or wine vinegar
  2 tablespoons butter
  200 g (7 ounces) gamalost, cubed

Combine sugar and vinegar and reduce over high heat to about 1 dl (1/2 cup). Beat in the butter. Stir in the cheese. Serve the cheese hot on crisp salad leaves. Use the remaining glaze as dressing.

Pultost is also good on lettuce with a vinaigrette dressing and whole-grain bread on the side.

Warm Lefse with Ham and Jarlsberg Cheese

Jarlsberg cheese is the flagship of Norwegian cheeses and is exported around the world. A wedge of mature flavorful Jarlsberg is a real treat. It's 100% Norwegian, first made at Jarlsberg manor in the last century. I like it best just as it is. When heated, it loses much of its special aroma, but the unique taste still remains.

Creamed Bell Peppers and Celery

4 dl (1 2/3 cups) finely chopped bell pepper
2 dl (3/4 cup) finely chopped celery
butter
2 dl (3/4 cup) whipping cream
freshly ground white pepper
2 tablespoons finely chopped parsley

Lefse for 4 Rolls

4 lefse or flour tortillas
4 large thick slices Jarlsberg cheese
4 slices boiled ham or tongue

Sauté the peppers and celery in butter until soft but not brown. Add cream and cook until thickened, 3-4 minutes. Sprinkle with parsley.

Preheat the oven to 150 °C (300 °F). Roll the lefse or tortillas around the cheese and ham. Pack in aluminum foil. Bake 10 minutes. Serve with creamed bell peppers and celery. Serves 4.

Livestock

Dairy products always have been our most important farm resource. Our traditional diet and our agricultural industry as a whole illustrate this. It is only since the second world war that livestock production has come to the forefront. The last 20 years have brought immense technical development in that field.

Consumers now demand better and more consistent quality in most things. We travel more and see things we want. The role of housewife has been downplayed here in Norway, which I feel is a shame. Too few children come home from school to the aroma of good food and a prepared dinner.

Years ago, many farms had sheep and goats. That isn't at all unusual, considering our landscape, with coastal and mountain regions throughout the country. Sheep, and especially goats, are moderate eaters and are satisfied with the sparse grasses on the mountainsides. In addition, sheep produce wool and leather for clothing, as well as milk and meat. Goats produce milk and heavy-duty leather. It was important that all parts of the animal be used.

Farms also kept chickens and pigs. Many legends about the pig date from preChristian times, and the pig has been the most appreciated animal in many ways. Most important, it was a source of fat, and fat was not so easy to obtain. People needed it, with all the hard physical labor.

A good pig was round, with a layer of fat along its back the width of a hand. And a pig was supposed to be big, not like the rather small but long and thin pigs we know today. Now, the tables are turned, and stockbreeders are concentrating on developing a pig with more marbling in the muscle. But, in days of old, the pig was the chief source of fat in the diet, and we can say that pork has the richest traditions in the

Norwegian kitchen. Even today, Norwegians appreciate pork more than any other type of meat. Half of all meat consumed in Norway is pork.

Luckily, we can see cows grazing outside during the summer all over Norway. In my home district, with its rich dairy traditions,

I know that the animals graze on mountain grasses for most of the summer season.

All of this reinforces our demands for quality in those animals which eventually will grace our dinner tables. It also reinforces our high aspirations, which will continue into the future.

All this illustrates that we want to set limits for technical development. We may soon be the last ones left in the world with these values.

Beef

In days of old, cattle were regarded as a source of meat only on large farms. The cow was kept for its milk, but after it no longer produced enough, it ended up in the stew pot. For that reason, many years could pass without beef on the table.

The female calf was the most valuable, because it could become a new milk producer. Calves were also easy to sell to other farmers. Male calves were set out to graze during the summer, but most people could not afford to feed an extra animal all winter, so they were slaughtered in the fall.

As mentioned earlier, Norway has its own cattle race, NRF. During the past few years, other races have come on the market, which are especially popular among chefs.

I feel that the grading of beef is very important, and our own meat producers have improved in that area. With proper grading, we can get just as good quality from our own NRF cattle as with specially bred beef cattle. And the best quality meat comes from cows.

We need quality in every step of production, so that the cook knows that his own high demands are met all the way to the kitchen counter. But the meat also has to be treated with care after it enters the kitchen.

All kinds of good dishes can be made from beef, and we all have our favorites. One advantage with beef is that fresh meat is available year-round. Everyone appreciates a good well-hung steak.

Brown Stock

4 kg (9 pounds) beef bones
2 onions
1 leek
3 carrots
1/4 celeriac or 3 stalks celery
water
6-7 bay leaves
1 1/2 teaspoons white peppercorns
1 teaspoon thyme
1 1/2 teaspoons salt

Preheat the oven to 225 °C (450 °F). Chop the bones into 5 cm (2") lengths. Cube the vegetables. Place the bones and vegetables in an oven pan with a little water in the bottom. Brown in the oven about an hour, turning often. There should always be a little water in the pan. Transfer to a pot and add water to cover. Bring slowly to a boil, skim, then add seasonings. Simmer 5-6 hours, skimming occasionally.

Strain and chill. Remove the fat and discard. If desired, reduce until more concentrated.

About Cooking Meat

Whether we are preparing a steak or a roast, a filet or a ptarmigan, we must remember that it is absolutely necessary to retain all the juices in the meat. For that reason, I like to roast in increments – alternately roasting and resting the meat for the same length of time. In that way, the juices are distributed throughout the piece of meat, making it tender and juicy. I think three increments are best, with the longest time first. The same technique can be used for steaming or braising.

All my meat recipes can be used with all types of meat. The burgers taste just as good with other meats as with beef.

Norwegian Burgers

This is a classic dish, based on knowledge and technique. Industry has not been kind to the burger, and many consumers have accepted the commercial burger without realizing that there is nothing like a homemade burger made from lean meat. I like to use arm, chuck and trimmings. Meat from the shank has a lot of gelatin in it, so the burgers don't fall apart so easily. This is a general recipe, which can be used with game, too.

1 kg (2 1/4 pounds) boneless beef
1 onion
2 teaspoons salt
1/2 teaspoon pepper
1 1/2 tablespoons potato starch
3 dl (1 1/4 cups) water, milk or cream
1 egg
clarified butter

Grind the meat together with the onion. Carefully blend in the salt and pepper. Alternately add potato starch and liquid, then mix in the egg. Let the mixture rest about 30 minutes before shaping into 80 g (3 ounce) patties. Fry in clarified butter or oil without burning. Since they continue to cook even after they are removed from the pan, do not fry until well-done. Serves 6-8.

Traditionally, these burgers are served with onions which have been sautéed until soft and shiny. I cannot bear burned onions, dry burgers and bad bread. Homemade burgers make a simple but delicious meal, always appreciated.

Filet of Beef with Celeriac Purée

Celeriac Purée

6 dl (2 1/2 cups) cubed celeriac
salt
water
2 tablespoons minced shallot or onion
freshly ground white pepper
1 tablespoon finely chopped basil

Sautéed Onions

2 onions, sliced
butter

Herbed Sour Cream

3 dl (1 1/4 cups) 35% fat sour cream
1 tablespoon finely chopped basil
1 tablespoon coarse grain mustard
2 tablespoons grated blue cheese

4 slices beef filet, about 180 - 200 g
   (6-7 ounces) each
clarified butter or oil
salt and freshly ground white pepper

Cook celeriac until tender in lightly salted water. Drain, then mash well. Combine with the shallots and cook 2-3 minutes, stirring constantly. Cool slightly, season with salt and pepper and stir in the basil.

Saute the onions in butter until golden and shiny.

Combine all ingredients for the herbed sour cream and beat until stiff. The mixture will become thin, then peak. Spoon onto the onions.

Preheat the oven to 225 °C (450 °F). Brown the steaks in clarified butter or oil until brown on all sides. Season with salt and pepper, then let rest 2-3 minutes. Place in the oven until they swell up a little, about 5 minutes. Remove from the oven, pack in foil and let rest 5 minutes.

Spoon the celeriac purée onto the steaks and place in the oven for 4-5 minutes. Serve with sautéed onions, herbed sour cream and baked potatoes. Serves 4.

Herb-Poached Filet of Beef Flavored with Rosemary

Preparing food for others is more than finding a good recipe. People often travel far to enjoy a good meal. The entire experience is important, the combination of taste, atmosphere and culture. This is a challenge to any cook, and in a restaurant, we define this as good service.

The basis for this dish is the big stew pot, which is part of our heritage. Now, few have time to use it anymore.

2 carrots
1 celeriac
2 onions
3 liters (quarts) rich beef stock
1 tablespoon chopped thyme
1 tablespoon chopped oregano
1 beef filet, about 1 1/2 kg (3 pounds)

Sauce:

1 1/2 liters (6 cups) beef stock
6 tablespoons chopped fresh rosemary
100 g (3 1/2 ounces, scant 1/2 cup)
   unsalted butter
salt

Clean the vegetables and cut into chunks. Add the vegetables to the stock with the herbs and bring to a boil. Trim the filet, removing all membrane. Cut into 3 pieces of approximately equal size and tie with cotton string. Place in the stock and simmer slowly 15-18 minutes. Remove from the stock and let rest 15 minutes. Then simmer an additional 10 minutes and let rest 10 minutes more.

Strain off 1 1/2 liters (6 cups) stock and place in a saucepan. Reduce over high heat until 1 liter remains. Add rosemary and simmer 15 minutes.

Return the meat to the stock pot and heat until warm, 3-4 minutes. Beat the butter into the rosemary-flavored stock. Cut the meat into even slices and serve on a bed of boiled root vegetables, such as onions, potatoes, carrots, parsley roots, and broccoli or spinach. Spoon the rosemary-flavored sauce over. Serves 8.

Poached Veal Tongue with Parsley Sauce

1 veal tongue
1 liter (quart) water
2 teaspoons salt
4-5 white peppercorns
2 carrots
1 leek
1 small celeriac
2 onions
100 g (3 1/2 ounces, scant 1/2 cup)
  unsalted butter
6 tablespoons flour
2 dl (3/4 cup) milk
salt and freshly ground white pepper
chopped parsley

Wash the tongue and place in a pot with the water. Bring to a boil, skim, then add salt and peppercorns. Simmer about 1 hour. Clean the vegetables, peel and add the peelings to the pot. Cut the onion into wedges, the other vegetables into cubes. Knead the butter and flour together.

Remove the tongue from the pot and peel off the skin. Whisk the butter-flour mixture gradually into the cooking liquid, then whisk in the milk. Add the vegetables and simmer until tender, about 15 minutes. Season with salt and pepper. Just before serving, sprinkle generously with chopped parsley. Slice the tongue and serve with sauce and vegetables.

Salad with Sautéed Kid Slices

Traditionally, kid is roasted in the oven until almost done, then splashed with cream and roasted 15-20 minutes more. That's the way my mother makes it, and it is a festive dish. I still can recommend this method.

I always choose or try to choose the cooking method which suits the ingredients.

This is not always easy, but often, simplest is best.

    1 leg of kid
    clarified butter or oil
    salt
    freshly ground white pepper
    2 small heads Boston or cos lettuce
    6 tablespoons chokecherry dressing
        or vinaigrette

Divide the leg at the knee and remove the large bone. Cut into 4 slices. Fry in clarified butter or oil about 3 minutes, turning often. Season with salt and pepper. Wash the lettuce and arrange on individual plates. Drizzle dressing over and top

with the meat. Serve with whole grain bread and butter. Serves 4.

Chokecherry Blossom Vinegar:

Pick chokecherry blossoms just when they start to bloom for the best taste and aroma.

Fill a glass with chokecherry blossoms. Pour over 4 parts vinegar, 1 part white wine. Seal, then refrigerate 2-3 weeks before using.

For salad dressing, mix with freshly squeezed orange juice and olive oil.

45

Lamb

Norwegians are proud of their lamb. Among chefs, it is the most respected and favored of locally produced meats. We know that Norwegian lamb is as good or better than any other in the world.

We also know that it is not good just because it is Norwegian. We have old traditions, sheep farmers are good at their work, and we have the right terrain for the animals. Mountain grazing provides not just good protein-rich food, but it also makes the animals exercise. All that climbing results in good fat marbling and well-developed muscles.

In addition, Norwegian sheep are thought to have developed from an ancient breed which originated along the Møre and Trøndelag coast. We don't know if our sheep today are descendants of these, although in one place they call are called stone age sheep. I think it is interesting that farmers are interested in preserving old breeds, so that everything isn't all the same after a while. Everyone has an opinion about what is best, but I like mountain lamb best.

We all looks forward to fresh lamb in the fall. That's not unusual, because just about everyone has heard of the quality of our own lamb. It is extra gratifying to know that many people are able to obtain fresh lamb.

We have many traditional recipes for mutton and lamb in Norway. These have achieved a new status recently. Dishes such as lamb and cabbage stew, lamb fricassee, smoked lamb heads, dried mutton ribs and sausages are traditions which deserve to be respected.

The most exciting thing about sheep is that they live outside, where they can graze on all the mountain and forest grasses, from early spring to late September.

Lamb Sweetbreads with Sweet and Sour Mushrooms

Sweetbreads have never been part of the traditional Norwegian kitchen, but they are a delicacy prepared in the right way.

400 g (14 ounces) lamb sweetbreads
1 liter (quart) water
1 carrot, in chunks
1 onion, in wedges
salt
6-7 white peppercorns
2 bay leaves

Sweet and Sour Mushrooms:

500 g (1 pound) fresh wild
    or domestic mushrooms
1 tablespoon clarified butter or oil
1 dl (1/3 cup) wine vinegar
    (preferably raspberry vinegar)
1 tablespoon sugar
1 dl (1/3 cup) apple juice
2 tablespoons finely chopped fresh herbs

Soak the sweetbreads in cold water 2-3 hours. Bring the water to a boil and add the vegetables and seasonings. Add the sweetbreads and simmer 20-25 minutes. Cool in the cooking liquid. Remove the sweetbreads and trim for fat and membrane.

Sweetbreads

about 400 g (14 ounces) cooked
    and cleaned sweetbreads
3-4 tablespoons clarified butter
salt and freshly ground white pepper

Sauté the mushrooms in butter or oil. Add vinegar, sugar and apple juice and simmer 2-3 minutes. Stir in the herbs.

Sauté the sweetbreads until brown in the butter. Season with salt and pepper. Arrange the sweet and sour mushrooms on a serving platter or individual dishes. Top with the sweetbreads. Serves 4.

Lamb and Crepe Casserole

800 g (1 3/4 pound) finely ground lamb
1 1/2 teaspoons salt
unsalted butter
4 thin unsweetened crepes,
  about 25 cm (10") in diameter
2 onions
6 tomatoes, peeled and seeded
2 teaspoons basil
freshly ground pepper
200 g (7 ounces, 5 dl, 2 cups) grated
  Jarlsberg cheese

Preheat the oven to 225 °C (425 °F)Mix the meat with the salt. Brush a 25 cm (10") spring-form with butter and place a crepe in the bottom. Spread a layer of meat all over it. Repeat until all crepes are covered. Chop the onions and tomatoes and sprinkle on top. Sprinkle with basil and pepper. Top with grated cheese. Bake about 40 minutes, until the cheese is bubbly and the meat is well done. Loosen the sides of the pan with a knife. Place on a platter and serve immediately. Serves 4-6.

47

Lightly Salted and Smoked Rack of Lamb with Creamed Root Vegetables

4 dl (1 2/3 cups) whipping cream
1 tablespoon coarse grain mustard
2 tablespoons chopped fresh thyme
150 g (5 ounces, 1 medium) potato, cubed
150 g (5 ounces, about 1/2 small)
  rutabaga, cubed
150 g (5 ounces, about 2 medium)
  carrots, cubed
150 g (5 ounces, about 1/2 large)
  celeriac, cubed
salt
1 lightly salted and smoked rack of lamb

Combine the cream, mustard and thyme and bring to a boil. Add the vegetables and cook until tender. By then, the cream should be almost evaporated and the mixture should hold together. Season with salt.

Place the meat on a rack in a pot and steam 8-10 minutes. Let rest 8-10 minutes. Then steam 4-5 minutes more and let rest 3-4 minutes.

Carve and serve on a bed of creamed vegetables. Serves 4.

Pork

The Norwegian pig is known around the world. As with our other animals, many countries want Norwegian breeding stock.

With us, pork has richer traditions than any other food, for many reasons. For many farmers, it was easy to raise pigs, and they grew quickly. In earlier times, the pig was the most important source of fat in the diet, but that is no longer the case today.

Extensive improvements in pig breeding have resulted in leaner and more homogeneous meat. We cooks feel that pork today is too lean, and breeders have, to a certain degree, succeeded in producing a more marbled meat, which will put it on restaurant menus again.

There are many traditional dishes made with pork. The following is one of my favorites, served in a more exciting way than usual.

Chopped Pork in Lefse with Sautéed Onion in Sour Cream

about 300 g (10 ounces) chopped pork
1 tablespoon butter
salt and white pepper
2 large onions, in wedges
oil or clarified butter
4 potato lefse (12-15 cm (5-6" diameter)
   or small flour tortillas
2-3 tablespoons 35% fat
   sour cream
1 tablespoon finely chopped
   fresh thyme

Brown the pork in the butter until completely cooked. Season with salt and pepper. Sauté the onion in oil or clarified butter until soft and golden. Divide the meat among the lefse or tortillas and wrap up like a package. Stir the sour cream and thyme into the onions and season, if necessary. Divide the creamed onions among 4 plates and top with the lefse rolls.

Serves 4 as an appetizer.
Tip: To hold the "packets" together, tie with blanched leek strips.

Roast Bacon with Rutabaga Purée

This is a favorite dish among the guests at Fossheim Hotel. Everyone seems to enjoy its smoky, salty flavor.

about 2 kg (4-5 pounds) lightly salted and smoked bacon, boneless, but with the rind

Preheat the oven to 150 °C (300 °F). Place the bacon on a rack over an oven pan. Score the rind. Add about 1 liter (quart) water to the pan. Bake about 90 minutes. Transfer the pan to the top oven shelf. Increase the temperature to 225 °C (425 °F) and roast until the rind is crispy, about 30 minutes. Be careful about using the grill, as the meat burns easily. Let the meat rest 10-15 minutes before carving. Serve with rutabaga purée. Serves 8-10.

Rutabaga Purée

1 1/2 kg (3 pounds) rutabagas
water
salt and freshly ground white pepper
3-4 tablespoons butter
1 dl (1/2 cup) milk
1/2 teaspoon ground nutmeg

Clean and cube the rutabaga. Cook until tender in water seasoned with salt and pepper. Drain, then mash or purée in a food processor with the butter and milk while still hot. Season with nutmeg. Serves 8–10.

Eggs and Poultry

Years ago, if poultry was mentioned, that meant hens, and hens produced eggs. And what is a kitchen without eggs?Unthinkable, fortunately.

Eggs are unique. It is impossible to describe fully their significance and uses. In all cases where one or more eggs are used, they have an effect on the rest of the ingredients, whether just fried sunny side up, in a cake, a sauce or a soufflé. The many proverbs involving chickens and eggs show that eggs have been appreciated since time immemorial. Everyone who could kept hens.

Now, when we speak of poultry, we think of chickens rather than hens. Grilled chicken has become a national dish. Production of chicken has been too standardized. After intense lobbying by many chefs, chickens have improved, as have other poultry products.

My views on ethical farming also extend to poultry. I feel that chickens should be allowed to run free, outside, using their instincts to grow in a natural way.

Smoked Chicken with Parsley Cream Sauce

Smoked meat and fish is popular and delicious. Most people who want meat or fish smoked take it to their local butcher, if they don't have their own smoker.

    1 chicken, about 1 1/2 kg (3 pounds)
    2-3 teaspoons salt

Sauce

    6 dl (2 1/2 cups) chicken stock
    1 bunch parsley
    1 onion, in wedges
    3 dl (1 1/4 cups) whipping cream
    salt

Remove the bag of giblets from the cavity of the chicken. Wash, removing excess fat, blood, kidneys, lungs plus any loose bits from the cavity and discard. Rinse and dry with paper towels. Bone the chicken, saving the bones for stock. Place legs-thighs and breasts on a platter and sprinkle with salt. Refrigerate overnight. Cold smoke. Bring the stock to a boil and add parsley stalks (save the leaves for later) and onion. Reduce over high heat to 3 dl (1 1/4 cups). Add cream and cook until the sauce thickens. Strain, discarding parsley stalks and onion. Blanch the parsley leaves, then chop. Stir into the sauce and season with salt. Preheat the oven to 175 °C (350 °F). Place the chicken in an oven pan and roast about 30 minutes. Let rest 3-4 minutes. Carve and serve with raw fried potatoes, parsley roots and cauliflower. Serves 4.

The Storehouse

To me, the storehouse is the symbol of our food culture, traditions and hospitality. Many larger farms had two or three storehouses for all the food which had to be stored through a long winter.

The size of the storehouse varied according to the size of the farm or plot of land. Poor tenant farmers (indentured for life) hardly needed a storehouse, has they had little or nothing to keep in it.

The building itself is always well-made, with detailed decoration. It is also practically constructed, to store things in the best possible way.

Modern times have all but eliminated the need for the storehouse. Many are now used for other than the original purpose. Others have been torn down. Fortunately, there are still many storehouses standing in Gudbrandsdal, especially in the northern part of the valley, in Sel, Vågå, Lom and Skjåk. Most are used as before, but with less variety than during the time when every farm ground its own flour and when salting and drying were the only ways to store meat.

The largest storehouse in the country is here in Lom. In books, it is mentioned as the biggest in northern Europe. I don't know which is the largest in the world. Originally it was used to store grain for Lom and Skjåk, and it stood by the parsonage. It is still standing just as it was built during the 1500's, about 500 years before Lillehammer Olympics.

A good storehouse has two floors and a turf roof. The turf insulates against the heat of the sun, so the temperature remains stable, even during the summer, especially on the first floor, where the hams are hung.

At Fossheim Hotel, we also have a storehouse, where we keep our own dried meats.

I have a little storehouse where I live. A farm without a storehouse is really lacking.

Salted and Dried Pork

Use an entire side of streaky bacon with even layering of meat and fat. Fat is needed for a good result.

    1 side of fresh streaky bacon with rind
    500 g (18 ounces, 6 dl, about 2 1/2 cups) sugar
    100 g (3 1/2 ounces, 3 dl, 1 1/4 cups) dried thyme and/or basil, crushed
    1 liter (quart) coarse salt

Remove all bones from the fresh bacon, then halve. Combine sugar and herbs and sprinkle half in the bottom of a container large enough to hold all the meat in a single layer. Place the meat on the herb mixture, rind side down, then sprinkle with the remaining herb mixture. Press down with a light weight and marinate 24 hours. Remove the meat. Make a layer of coarse salt in the bottom of the container. Top with the meat, rind side down. Pack with coarse salt. Marinate 10 days, then brush off the salt and hang in a cool, airy place. After 6-8 weeks, it should be ready.

Dried Reindeer or Beef Heart

This recipe can be used for any kind of heart.

Butterfly the heart and wash well. Cover with coarse salt and refrigerate 24 hours. (Beef hearts need 48 to 72 hours). Hang the heart in an airy, insect-free place from two to four weeks, depending upon the size of the heart and the humidity.

Dried Ham

In my district, we have the optimal conditions to make good dried meats. A dry, stabile climate is absolutely necessary. It is therefore difficult to give directions for salting and drying for other parts of the country, but I'll try.

A good dried ham is hard to find. For a ham to dry properly, it has to go through a long process, and that takes six to seven months. Dried ham isn't uniquely Norwegian. Most countries have their own special dried meats, not really unlike our own. But in contrast to us, many countries in southern Europe have managed to produce these delicacies on a large scale, while maintaining high standards of both workmanship and quality.

Views regarding what makes a dried ham good are just as many as in all other traditional preparations. Everyone has a different opinion. I learned mostly from my father, and he from his father. Even so, not all my hams are successful.

The traditional time to make ham is in the fall, when the pigs are slaughtered, and the weather is just right for the task.

A whole ham, from the leg or the shoulder, weighing between 12 and 15 kilo (26-32 pounds), is about right. It should be very fresh and should not have been lying around either under or over other pieces of meat. Carve out the shoulder or hip bone and trim the edges of any loose bits. Dry the meat well. Rub with sugar and lots of coarsely crushed peppercorns.

Pour a layer of coarse salt into the bottom of a large, deep tray or other container big enough to contain the entire cut of meat. Arrange the ham on the salt, then cover completely with salt. Marinate 3 1/2 days per kilo (40 hours per pound) meat. So, if the ham weighs 12 kilos (26 pounds), it should marinate about 6 weeks.

Check that no brine appears, and make sure that the salt is against the meat and doesn't just form a crust over it.

When the ham is salted, hang in a cool, airy place (barn, attic with adequate air circulation).

A refrigerator is too cold. By May, the ham should be ready to eat.

My favorite ham is packed in canvas and then "buried" in barley grain for at least six months more.

Cold Storage

The coldest place in a house was usually the cellar. Often the cellar of a house or storehouse was used for cold storage. In some places, part of a house was built underground or into a hill to be used for cold storage.

A cold storage room should be well below ground level and should have stone walls and an earthen floor. This allows for the best storage possibilities, with even temperature, frostfree in winter and cool in summer. Milk products, berries, jam, juice, vegetables and canned goods were stored there.

Many methods of preparation are being forgotten. This is a shame, for many give much better results than freezing. In addition, it is much nicer to have rows of jars filled with all kinds of fruits and conserves than lots of convenience foods packed into a freezer.

Fermented Trout

Fermented trout is part of the soul of Norwegian food traditions. Fermented fish is a "must" at Christmas for most of us. Fermenting is a traditional method of storing fish, developed over decades, before modern preservation methods were known.

In many places fish were plentiful. It was common to prepare this kind of fish in large quantities, to sell before Christmas. For many families, it was a good way to earn extra money. Most fish which was fermented was caught in late summer or in the fall. It was prepared while fresh and matured until Christmas. This was a seasonal dish which developed into a tradition on many Christmas tables.

Trout is the most popular fish for fermenting, but whitefish also is used. I can't tell you which is best, for it's a matter of preference.

There are as many recipes for fermented fish as there are opinions about it. I like it best before it gets too strong. It should be mild and firm, but also spreadable. It should not be too salty.

Many are afraid of botulism poisoning from fermented fish. The story about the cat on the stairs has spread throughout the country. This fear sits firmly in us and dates from long ago. People always knew that the fish should not be placed on the ground. They didn't know why, but they knew that it was dangerous. Today we know that temperature plays an important role. Fish which are stored at 4-6 °C (40-43 °F) are completely safe. Fermented fish can be stored at a slightly higher temperature, but I think it matures best at the lower temperature.

It is best to ferment fresh fish, but it is possible to use frozen fish, too. If you want to try making fermented fish, but you haven't caught any, buy small farmed trout, about 300-500 g (10-18 ounces) each.

Clean the fish well. Remove the gills and rinse several times. Dry with paper towels. Use a clean wooden or plastic bucket for fermentation.

Be careful to use the correct amount of salt. It should be about 5% of the amount of fish. An old rule is to put as much salt in the cavity as there is room in the head of the fish.

Use the method described below to make fermented fish.

Fermented Fish

Fermented fish, *rakefisk,* is a delicacy, but even for some Norwegians, it is an acquired taste.

Use very fresh fish. Wash well and rinse in several changes of water. Dry with paper towels. The fish must be completely free of blood. Layer fish in a small wooden barrel with the cavities diagonally upward. Sprinkle a tablespoon of salt and a teaspoon of sugar on each layer. Place a weight on top and let stand 48-72 hours, the first day at room temperature, to start the fermentation process. Then refrigerate. Keep the lid tightly fastened. After 48 or 72 hours, a brine will form. If it does not cover the fish completely, make additional brine by bringing 3 liters (quarts) water, 1 dl (1/2 cup) salt and 2 teaspoons sugar to a boil. Cool the brine completely, then pour it over the fish.

The fish is ready after 5-8 weeks. It is important to change the brine if it becomes cloudy or turns brown. Use the above recipe. *Rakefisk* is served with lefse or flatbread and butter.

Canned Blueberries

2 kg (4 1/2 pounds) ripe blueberries
1 liter (quart) water
450 g (1 pound, 5 dl, 2 cups) sugar

Preheat the oven to 100 °C (210 °F). Clean the berries well. Place in clean jars. Bring the water and sugar to a boil. Simmer 2-3 minutes. Pour over the berries. Seal. Place in the oven for 30 minutes. Serve as a dessert with vanilla sauce (see recipe, page 14).

This recipe can be used with all kinds of wild berries.

Red Currant-Mint Jam

Red currants grow all over Norway. Even if you don't have them in your garden, you can buy them for a reasonable price.

1 kg (2 1/4 pounds, 12 dl, 5 cups) sugar
2 dl (3/4 cup) water
1 vanilla bean
1 kg (2 1/4 pounds) cleaned berries
1 tablespoon finely chopped mint

Bring the sugar and water to a boil with the vanilla bean and simmer 5 minutes. Add the berries and simmer 5-10 minutes. Strain the berries and reduce the juice by half over high heat. Transfer the berries to jars and add the mint. Pour over the concentrated juice. Seal.

Pickled Mushrooms

1 liter (quart) mixed wild mushrooms, cleaned and quartered
3 dl (1 1/4 cups) 7% apple cider vinegar
1 1/2 dl (2/3 cup) sugar
7-8 white peppercorns
5 allspice berries
1 bay leaf

Place the mushrooms in clean jars. Combine remaining ingredients and bring to a boil. Pour the boiling brine over the mushrooms. Seal immediately.

Pickled Rutabaga

1 kg (2 1/4 pounds) rutabaga,
  in 1 cm (6/16") cubes
1 liter (quart) water
1 tablespoon salt
7 dl (3 cups) 7% vinegar
500 g (18 ounces, 6 dl, 2 1/2 cups) sugar
1 dill crown per glass

Cook the rutabaga cubes until tender in the water with the salt. Drain, then transfer to clean jars. Bring the vinegar and sugar to a boil, then pour over the rutabaga cubes. Place a dill crown in each jar. Seal. Store in a cold, dark place.

Lingonberry-Chokecherry Juice Concentrate

This is an old recipe. Sometimes pure choke-cherry juice is too strong, so it is good to add lingonberries.

2 liters (quarts) chokecherries
4 liters (1 gallon) lingonberries
4 liters (1 gallon) water
300 g (10 1/2 ounces, 3 3/4 dl, 1 1/2 cups)
   sugar per liter juice concentrate

Crush the chokecherries. Combine with the lingonberries in a pot. Add water and bring to a boil. Simmer 15 minutes. Strain through a juice cloth, pressing all liquid from the fruit. Measure and add sugar accordingly. Bring to a boil, skimming, if necessary. Pour into clean bottles. Seal.

Spiced Whisky

I have experimented with the many different herbs which grow in the hills near my home.

1/2 liter (2 cups) vodka
1/2 liter (2 cups) aquavit
1 piece angelica root
100 g (3 1/2 ounces, 2 1/2 dl, 1 cup)
   lingonberries
2 tablespoons light brown sugar

Combine all ingredients and store for a month before straining and bottling.

Chokecherry-Lingonberry Whisky or Liqueur

This combination is good for both whisky and liqueur.

Whisky

1 liter (quart) crushed chokecherries
1 liter (quart) lingonberries
50 g (1 3/4 ounce, 4 tablespoons, 1/4 cup)
   light brown sugar
2 bottles vodka or cognac

Combine and pour into clean bottles. Seal and age one month before using.

Liqueur

1 liter (quart) crushed chokecherries
1 liter (quart) lingonberries
1 kg (2 1/4 pounds, 12 dl, 5 cups) sugar
2 bottles vodka

Follow the directions for whisky.

The bakehouse

In the traditional farm complex, the bakehouse had a natural place. Several times a year, great quantities of bread of different types, which could withstand long storage, were made.

There were a good many kinds of bread, many of which still are baked. Today, flatbread and lefse are the best known sorts.

Some people are better at making these breads than others. Long ago, baker ladies went from farm to farm baking, especially before Christmas and other special days.

You should never discuss bread with a baker. Seldom do two bake bread in the same way, which is why it is difficult to give recipes, when each little area has its own traditions.

Not only should sweets served with coffee taste good, they should look good, too. Both creativity and handiwork go into making a good cake table. There's a great variety here, but some have more history than others.

The most important from my district are two kinds of wafers, cones and rosettes.

"Unni Bread"

50 g (1 3/4 ounces) fresh yeast
  (or 12 g (4 teaspoons) dry yeast)
1 liter (quart) lukewarm water
2 dl (3/4 cup) sunflower seed kernels
1 dl (1/2 cup) linseeds
1 dl (1/2 cup) sesame seeds
2 dl (3/4 cup) oatmeal
2 dl (3/4 cup) cracked wheat
1 teaspoon salt
1 1/2 liters (6 1/2 cups) flour

Dissolve the yeast in the warm water. Add seeds, oats, cracked wheat and salt. Work in the flour to make a stiff dough. Let rise in a warm place 30-45 minutes. Knead well and divide into thirds. Place in loaf pans and let rise 60-90 minutes. Preheat the oven to 190 °C (375 °F). Bake 50 minutes.

Bread Rolls

I always serve fresh bread or rolls with all my menus. I normally use Skjåk flour, which is barley flour made from grain grown in the Otta valley and ground in the mill at Skjåk.

Bread should be good, and it is always easier to get good bread with good flour. I often wonder why Norwegian consumers are so complacent about bread. It seems to be only the price that counts. But, many bake at home, fortunately, and lately new and better breads are appearing in the shops.

Coates Bakery in Moss makes a bread which bears my name, and of course, Skjåk flour is an important ingredient. That recipe is, naturally, a secret, but here is a recipe for rolls made with Skjåk or barley flour.

100 g (3 1/2 ounces) fresh yeast
1 l (scant 5 cups) cold water
100 g (3 1/2 ounces, scant 1/2 cup) butter
2 teaspoons salt
2 eggs
18 dl (7 1/2 cups) flour
5 dl (2 cups) barley flour

Dissolve the yeast in the water. Melt the butter and add along with the salt and eggs. Gradually add the flour (setting aside a little for the second kneading), kneading well, until the dough is smooth and elastic. Cover and let rise in a warm place until double, about an hour. Knead until smooth, using more flour if needed. Form into rolls. Let rise until double, about 45 minutes. Preheat the oven to 200 °C (400 °F). Bake 30 minutes.

Christmas Cake

1 kg (2 1/4 pounds, 2 liters, 8 cups) flour
200 g (7 ounces, 2 1/2 dl, 1 cup) sugar
1/2 teaspoon cardamom
150 g (5 ounces, 1/2 cup + 2 tablespoons)
  margarine
50 g (1 3/4 ounces) fresh yeast
6 dl (2 1/2 cups) lukewarm milk
130 g (4 1/2 ounces, 2 dl, 3/4 cup) raisins
50 g (1 3/4 ounces, scant dl, 1/3 cup)
  chopped citron
1 egg
2 tablespoons water

Sift the flour with the sugar and cardamom. Crumble in the margarine. Dissolve the yeast in the milk and add. Knead until smooth and elastic. Cover and let rise in a warm place until doubled, about an hour. Knead in the raisins and citron.

Divide into thirds and form round loaves. Let rise in a warm place until doubled, about 45 minutes.

Preheat the oven to 180 °C (350 °F). Combine egg and water and brush over the loaves. Bake about 1 hour.

Cone Cookies (Skryllo)

The people around Otta distinguish between *krumkaker* and *skryllo,* even though both are made in the same iron. Traditionally, recipes containing eggs are called *krumkaker,* while those containing cream are called *skryllo.*

1/2 liter (2 cups) whipping cream
4 tablespoons (1/4 cup) sugar
4 dl (1 2/3 cups) flour
1/2 teaspoon vanilla extract

Lightly whip the cream. Stir in the remaining ingredients. Bake in a *krumkake* or pizzelle iron and form into cones while still warm.

Simple Wafers

These wafers appear throughout the year on coffee tables, much like cone cookies. These wafers are usually eaten plain with coffee, but they also can be spread with butter and cheese for a more hearty snack. They usually are served on a plate which is just the right size to fit their diameter of 15 cm (6").

500 g (1 pound, 2 cups) shortening
250 g (8 ounces, 1 cup) margarine
1 egg
2 dl (3/4 cup) milk
250 g (8 ounces, 2 1/4 dl, 1 cup) sugar
1/2 teaspoon hornsalt
   (or 1 tablespoon baking powder)

1 teaspoon cardamom
1 1/4 kg (2 3/4 pounds, 2 1/2 liters, 10-11 cups) flour

Cream the shortening with the margarine. Beat the egg with the milk. Mix the remaining ingredients. Add milk and flour mixtures alternately to the fat. You might want to set aside a small amount of flour for rolling out. Roll out with a patterned rolling pin, then cut into 15 cm (6") circles with a pastry or pizza cutter. Bake on a griddle, patterned side first, over medium heat. Each round should cook 6-7 minutes, or they will be soft.

Wafers

Wafers are served with coffee and with sour cream porridge, or even with a good dessert. In my local area, a coffee table without these wafers is unthinkable.

Many homes still have old wafer irons with long handles for holding them over the fire. Now it is possible to buy wafer irons to use on top of the stove. Local craftsmen continue the tradition of these irons, which have a special pattern.

It is also possible to make wafers on a *krumkake* or pizzelle iron.

3 dl (1 1/4 cups) whipping cream

3 dl (1 1/4 cups) sour cream
1 1/4 dl (1/2 cup) water
salt
barley flour or regular flour

Combine the two creams, then add the remaining ingredients. The kind of flour used is a matter of personal preference. In the old days, barley flour was easier to get, but now most use regular flour. Make the batter a little thicker than for waffles. It is very important for the iron not to be too hot. It is a slow process to make these wafers, because they must dry out as well as cook.

Rosettes

This is an especially decorative cookie for any coffee table. Rosette irons can be bought in specialty shops. In our district, there are many old irons with different patterns.

2-3 eggs
2 dl (3/4 cup) milk
1 1/2 tablespoons sugar
80 g (3 ounces, 1 1/2 dl, 2/3 cup) flour

1/4 teaspoon vanilla sugar
(or 1/8 teaspoon extract)
oil or shortening

Combine all ingredients except oil. Heat the oil. Dip the iron into the batter and immediately plunge it into the hot oil. It is hot enough when the cookie leaves the iron almost immediately. Cook until golden. Drain on paper towels.

Lingonberry Cake

Barley flour gives extra flavor to a sponge cake.

6 eggs
200 g (7 ounces, 2 1/2 dl, 1 cup) sugar
100 g (3 1/2 ounces, 2 dl, 3/4 cup)
   barley flour
80 g (3 ounces, 1 1/4 dl, 1/2 cup)
   potato starch (or cornstarch)
2 tablespoons flour
1 teaspoon baking powder

Filling:

500 g (18 ounces) fresh or thawed
   lingonberries
3 tablespoons sugar
2 teaspoons vanilla sugar
1 liter (quart) whipping cream
4 tablespoons sugar

Preheat the oven to 175 °C (350 °F). Grease a 26 cm (10") springform or round, straight-sided cake pan. Beat eggs and sugar until light and lemon-colored. Combine the dry ingredients and fold into the egg mixture. Pour into the pre-pared pan. Bake on the lowest oven shelf about 45 minutes. Cool completely, then divide hori-zontally into two or three layers.

Reserve about 1/3 of the berries for garnish. Mash the rest with the first amount of sugar and vanilla sugar. Whip the cream with the remain-ing sugar. Stir a little mashed berries into the cream. Spread a layer of berry-cream over the bottom layer, top with another layer, repeating until all but a small amount of cream is used. Sprinkle the top of the cake with the reserved berries, and pipe the remaining cream around the edge of the cake.

Note: Cranberries can substituted for lingon-berries, but they require an extra step. They are about twice the size of lingonberries and must be cooked first. Do not reserve any for garnish. Chop 1 pound (450 g) cranberries, combine with 1/2 cup (1 1/4 dl) sugar (3 tablespoons is not enough) and cook 5-8 minutes, until soft and semi-puréed. Stir in the vanilla, then whip cream, etc.

According to tradition, we have been self-sufficient for most things, and that means we like to have a garden with berries, fruit, herbs and vegetables. For many, this has developed into a profession or an additional income. I am thinking about fruit and berry growing, in particular.

We know that berries and fruit which thrive here, in spite of a short, hectic summer, are of top quality. This is due to the long light days so far north. So much light gives the fruit a unique character. In addition, there is very little spraying, usually none at all, and the earth is good and clean.

The latter means a lot in my kitchen. That we have an honest natural basis for my handiwork makes me proud as a cook.

The sweet conclusion to a meal is often the weak side of a chef. Usually, desserts are the domain of the pastry chef. After being neglected for a long time, this profession is making a comeback. It is true that only a few hotels and restaurants can have a pastry chef, but the big ones ought to have a good pastry chef on their payroll.

In Norway, we have many personalities in the profession who are respected internationally. My favorite is Lars Lian, who can be found at Erichsen's Konditori in Trondheim. I worked with him on the national culinary team, which won two silver medals in the Culinary Olympics in 1992, one in pastry, and with courses at Fossheim.

Here is one of his recipes.

Chocolate Roll with Rhubarb Sauce and Cinnamon Sorbet

40 g (1 1/3 ounces, 3 1/2 tablespoons) flour
15 g (1/2 ounce, 2 1/2 tablespoons) cocoa
40 g (1 1/3 ounces, 2/3 dl, 1/4 cup)
   confectioner's sugar
40 g (1 1/3 ounces, 2 tablespoons +
   1 teaspoon) soft butter

40 g (1 1/3 ounces, 2 1/2 tablespoons)
   egg white

Sift the flour, cocoa and sugar together. Beat the butter, then add the flour mixture and the egg white. Fill into a small paper pastry bag. Cut a tiny hole in the bag and pipe a lattice pattern on a length of parchment paper which has been cut to the size of a baking sheet. Freeze flat until stiff, 10-15 minutes. While this is freezing, make the cake.

    100 g (3 1/2 ounces, 2 size 3 or "large") eggs
    35 g (3 tablespoons) sugar
    40 g (1 1/3 ounces, 4 1/2 tablespoons)
        sifted flour
    coffee syrup (1 dl [1/3 cup] each
        strong coffee, water and sugar)

Preheat the oven to 240 °C (450 °F). With an electric mixer, beat eggs and sugar until light and lemon-colored. Add the flour, beating at the highest speed for a short time. Remove the latticework from the freezer and carefully spread the batter over it. It will be a very thin layer. Bake about 7 minutes, until lightly golden. Turn out and cool. Drizzle with coffee syrup, if desired.

Chocolate Cream

    1 vanilla bean
    1 1/4 dl (1/2 cup) 2% fat milk
    1 dl (scant 1/2 cup) whipping cream
    40 g (3 1/2 tablespoons) sugar
    15 g (1/2 ounce, 2 tablespoons) cornstarch
    3 egg yolks
    100 g (3 1/2 ounces) bittersweet or
        semi-sweet chocolate
    3 1/2 dl (1 1/3 cups) whipping cream

Split the vanilla bean and scrape out the tiny seeds in the middle. Combine the milk and cream. Add the vanilla bean with seeds and the sugar. Bring to a boil. Whisk the cornstarch with the egg yolks until completely dissolved. Whisk in the boiling milk mixture, then return to the pan and bring to a boil, whisking constantly.

Break the chocolate into small pieces and add. Stir until melted. Cool. Whip the cream and fold into the chocolate cream. Spread the cream over the cake and roll up. Freeze. Cut the cake when frozen.

Rhubarb Sauce

    500 g (1 pound) rhubarb
    5 dl (2 cups) water
    225 g (8 ounces, 2 1/2 dl, 1 cup) sugar
    1 vanilla bean, split lengthwise
    20 g (3/4 ounce, 1 1/2 tablespoons) honey
    15 g (1/2 ounce, 2 tablespoons) cornstarch
    2 tablespoons cold water

Clean half the rhubarb, cut into small dice and set aside. Clean the remaining rhubarb and cut into chunks. Place, along with the trimmings in a saucepan with the water, sugar, vanilla bean and honey. Bring to a boil and simmer 7-8 minutes. Stir together cornstarch and water and add. Add the reserved diced rhubarb to the boiling sauce. Cool.

Cinnamon Sorbet

    200 g (7 ounces, 2 1/4 dl, 1 scant cup) sugar
    5 dl (2 cups) sweet sparkling wine,
        cider or apple juice
    2 cinnamon sticks
    105 g (3 3/4 ounces, 1 dl, scant 1/2 cup)
        glucose

Simmer sugar, water and syrup 5 minutes. Add glucose and bring to a boil. Cool, then freeze in an ice cream machine.

Cookie Baskets

    50 g (6 1/2 tablespoons) flour
    50 g (5 tablespoons) confectioner's sugar
    1 egg
    pinch cinnamon

Preheat the oven to 200 °C (400 °F). Sift flour and sugar. Mix in the egg. Spread the batter over a 7 cm (3") round template on a greased baking sheet. Bake until light golden, about 5minutes. Immediately after removing from the oven, drape over a cup to form a small basket.

Serve the chocolate cake roll with rhubarb sauce, cinnamon sorbet in the cookie basket, fresh berries, orange zest and mint leaves.

71

Red Currant Cake with Sour Cream

Sponge base

3 eggs
60 g (2 ounces, 1/4 cup) sugar
50 g (6 1/2 tablespoons) flour
30 g (2 tablespoons) butter,
  melted and cooled

2-3 tablespoons red currant wine or port wine

Filling

5 dl (2 cups) sour cream
2 dl (3/4 cup) coarsely chopped
  hazelnuts or walnuts
1 tablespoon finely chopped mint

Garnish

8 sheets gelatin
5-6 dl (2-2 1/4 cups) crushed red currants

Preheat the oven to 180 °C (350 °F). Grease a 24 cm (10") springform. Beat the eggs and sugar until light and lemon-colored. Fold in the flour, then the butter. Pour into the prepared pan and bake 12 minutes. Cool in the pan. Sprinkle the cake with the wine. Beat the sour cream until stiff. Fold in the nuts and mint. Pour into the pan. Soak the gelatin in cold water to soften, about 5 minutes. Squeeze excess water from the gelatin sheets and melt. Fold thoroughly into the crushed black currants. Pour carefully over the sour cream layer. Refrigerate 1-2 hours.

Nut Cake with Plums and Troll Cream

Nut Cake

8 egg whites
400 g (14 ounces, 5 dl, 2 cups) sugar
400 g (14 ounces, 9 dl, 4 cups)
  ground hazelnuts
1 teaspoon vanilla sugar
  (or 1/2 teaspoon vanilla extract)

1 kg (2 pounds) plums

Preheat the oven to 230 °C (425 °F). Grease a 25 cm (10") springform. Beat the egg whites until almost stiff. Gradually add the sugar and beat to a stiff meringue. Fold in the nuts and vanilla sugar. Pour into the prepared pan. Bake until light brown but still soft, 30-40 minutes. Cool the cake in the pan. Lower the heat to 170 °C (350 °F).

Scald the plums by dipping in boiling water. The peel should slip right off. Divide lengthwise and remove the pit. Arrange on the cake.

Troll Cream

8 egg whites
2 tablespoons sugar
2 teaspoons vanilla sugar (or 1 teaspoon
  vanilla extract)
5 dl (2 cups) lingonberries

Beat the egg whites until soft peaks form. Add the sugar and vanilla sugar and beat until stiff. Fold in the berries. For a pink dessert, beat the berries with the egg whites. Pour over the plums. Bake about 10 minutes, until golden. Cool before serving. Note: Cooked, puréed cranberries can be substituted for lingonberries.

Blueberry Ice Cream with Pernod and Vanilla

This is really a parfait. This word refers to the handiwork in the making of the dessert. Other flavorings can be used.

1 vanilla bean, split lengthwise
2 dl (3/4 cup) water
2 dl (3/4 cup) pernod
200 g (7 ounces, 2 1/4 dl, 1 scant cup) sugar
8 egg yolks
3 dl (1 1/4 cups) blueberry juice or purée
3 dl (1 1/4 cups) whipping cream

Combine vanilla bean, water, pernod and sugar in a saucepan. Bring to a boil and reduce until half the original amount remains. Remove the vanilla bean and save. Beat the egg yolks in a deep bowl. Place the bowl over a pot of boiling water, add the pernod syrup and beat until creamy. Beat in the blueberry juice. Place the bowl in a pan of cold water and beat until cold. Whip the cream and fold in.

Pour into a mold and freeze.

Black Currant Cream in a Cup

Few berries have as rich a flavor as the black currant. Most black currants are made into juice, but many different desserts can be made with this berry. While most desserts are served on dishes, this one is served warm in a cup.

6 dl (2 1/2 cups) whipping cream
200 g (7 ounces, 2 1/4 dl, 1 scant cup) sugar
4 dl (1 2/3 cups) black currant purée
  (see recipe for strawberry puree, page 75)

1 tablespoon finely chopped mint
10 eggs

Preheat the oven to 110 °C (230 °F). Bring cream and sugar to a boil. Add black currant purée and mint and return to the boil. Beat the eggs, then add the boiling liquid, beating constantly. Strain and pour into 10 cups. Bake, preferably in a fan oven for about 20 minutes. Serve immediately. The cream will be soft. Serves 10.

Crispy Nut Waffles with Egg Cream and Strawberries

For this dessert to be really good, the waffles should be freshly made and still crispy.

    100 g (3 1/2 ounces, scant 1/2 cup) butter
    2 1/2 dl (1 cup) water
    3 1/2 dl (1 1/2 cups) flour
    2 dl (3/4 cup) milk
    2 teaspoons baking powder
    2 dl (3/4 cup) chopped hazelnuts

Melt the butter, then cool. Combine the remaining ingredients well, then add the butter. Grease the iron for the first waffle. Bake until golden and serve immediately. Makes 10.

Egg Cream

    5-6 egg yolks
    125 g (4 1/2 ounces, 1 1/4 dl, 1/2 cup) sugar
    40 g (1 1/2 ounces, 3/4 dl, 1/3 cup) flour
    1/4 teaspoon salt
    6 dl (2 1/2 cups) milk
    1 vanilla bean, split lengthwise

Whisk egg yolks and sugar until thick. Whisk in the flour, a little at a time, then the salt.

Combine milk and vanilla bean in a saucepan and bring to a boil. Whisk into the beaten egg yolk mixture. Return to the saucepan and whisk until it returns to a boil. Simmer 2 minutes. Strain, then cool. For a fluffier cream, add whipped cream or beaten egg whites.

Serve with strawberries and strawberry purée. Count on 1 1/2 baskets of strawberries for 6 servings. Clean the berries and quarter. Place a waffle heart on a dish and top with egg cream. Spoon strawberries over the cream and top with another waffle heart. Sprinkle with confectioner's sugar and garnish with mint or lemon verbena. Spoon strawberry purée around the waffles.

Strawberry Purée

1 1/2 baskets strawberries, about 750 g (1 2/3 pounds), or other berries
juice of 1/2 lemon
1 tablespoon confectioner's sugar

Clean the berries and purée with the lemon juice and confectioner's sugar in a blender or food processor. Sieve. If too thick, thin with a little cold sugar syrup.

Cloudberry Soufflé

From early August, all kinds of berries are just waiting to be picked in the woods and mountains. Remember not to pick unripe berries. On the whole, the berries in Norwegian forests are a little used resource. Only a small percentage of the entire production is used. But, we buy berries, juice and jam from countries which we know have lots of pollution.

We must define the word quality for the next generation. It seldom has any connection with price. While berries and other useful plants are rotting, people use less and less money on food, soon only 15% of income. In this way, the affluent society has gone too far.

With a little initiative, you can collect nature's bounty for your breakfast table, dessert, juice and much more. The resources are there, and they cost nothing.

Cloudberries are the gold of the mountains. No other berry receives so much attention.

Many feel that this is undeserved. One reason these berries are so desirable is that some years they are very scarce. They grow in the border regions for cultivating fruit, and if an early frost kills the flowers, then what little is left becomes desirable. One thing we know is that foreigners do not appreciate cloudberries because of all the seeds. For that reason, it is good to use them in dishes where the berries are sieved.

3 dl (1 1/4 cups) cloudberry purée
1 dl (scant 1/2 cup) cloudberry liqueur
60 g (2 ounces, 3/4 dl, 1/3 cup) sugar
6 eggs, separated
1 tablespoon cornstarch
butter
sugar

Preheat the oven to 200 °C (400 °F). Whisk the cloudberry purée with the liqueur, sugar and egg yolks in a double boiler. Whisk until light and fluffy. Beat the egg whites with the cornstarch until stiff and fold into the berry mixture.

Grease 4 large individual soufflé forms with butter and sprinkle with sugar. Divide the batter among the forms. Bake 15 minutes. Serve immediately.

Finger Food

Small open face sandwiches are served around the world. They are considered finger food. How this expression came about, I don't know, but it is appropriate and used frequently.

I don't know why I hear the expression so much now. Whether it is a good one, I don't know, but it is liberating, and it gives the cook the possibility of serving a simple meal in accord with our own identity and traditions.

Norwegian food and culture is coming along, and fortunately, Norwegian chefs are being used to a greater degree for presentations and events, both at home and abroad.

A meal doesn't have to be formal, and you don't have to sit at a table for a long time for it to be good. Whatever kind of arrangement there is, there should be good food. I have used finger food on many special occasions.

When Queen Sonja laid the cornerstone for the Norwegian Mountain Museum in Lom during the summer of 1992, I served finger food in a 300-year-old building in Presthaugen in Lom, right where the museum will be. The theme for the finger food was, of course, the mountains and food for the elves.

Later that year, I also made finger food when the queen opened the new painting collection in Lillehammer. On many other occasions, I have used finger food for special receptions for many guests, where lack of space and other practical things made formal service impossible.
This can be done at home, too. When we invite guests, we want to serve something both good and somewhat unusual. So finger food is also appropriate for the home kitchen, where the hosts can apply their imagination to familiar ingredients. Although the food is simple, some advance work has to be done. There also should be a certain amount of handiwork, concern and innovation in such a spread.

For most people, it is a pleasant change to sample different tastes and kinds of food on various platters, and at the same time discuss the food and the flavors with others.

Whole-Grain Bread with Marinated Reindeer Filet and Berry Yogurt

See the recipe on page 106 for marinated reindeer filet. Other meat also can be prepared in the same way.

1 dl (1/2 cup) 35% fat sour cream
2 dl (1 cup) mixed berry yogurt
whole-grain bread
butter
500 g (1 pound) marinated reindeer filet

Beat the sour cream until stiff (it first becomes thin, then it peaks) and fold in the yogurt. Cut the bread into thin slices. Butter lightly, then quarter each slice. Slice the meat paper-thin on the diagonal and form into a rosette on each piece of bread. Spoon a little sour cream into the middle. Garnish with lingonberries, if desired.

Arrange on a serving platter, even on a stone slab or old wooden tray. Don't overload the dishes, rather add as they become depleted.

Flatbread with Blue Cheese Cream

Blue Cheese Cream

3 dl (1 1/4 cups) 35% fat sour cream
150 g (5 ounces) blue cheese, grated
1 tablespoon finely chopped fresh thyme

Combine sour cream and grated cheese. Stir in the thyme. Spoon onto pieces of flatbread or unsalted crackers and garnish with additional chopped fresh herbs.

Lefse with Jarlsberg Cheese, Ham and Coarse Mustard

Roll lefse or flour tortillas around thin slices of cheese and ham spread with coarse grain mustard. Cut into short lengths and hold together with cocktail picks.

Fermented Fish Mousse with Lefse

100 g (3 ounces, 1 small) onion
1 dl (1/3 cup) aquavit
250 g (8 ounces) boneless fermented
  or smoked fish
1/2 teaspoon freshly ground white pepper
4 lefse, about 20 cm (8") square,
  or flour tortillas

Chop the onion and place in a food processor with the aquavit and fish. Purée, then add pepper. Spread on the lefse, then stack.

Cut into squares and garnish with pickled vegetables held on with cocktail picks.

Smoked Salmon Mousse in Lefse

300 g (10 ounces) smoked salmon or trout
1 dl (1/3 cup) dark beer
2-3 tablespoons 35% fat sour cream
3-4 lefse or flour tortillas

Cut the salmon into chunks and place in a food processor with the beer and sour cream. Purée. Spread on the lefse, roll up and slice. Fasten with cocktail picks and serve with herbspiked aquavit.

Supplements from Nature
Wilderness Resources

The resources of nature have been the basis for settlement all over the country. The first who came were hunters. Even after Norwegians became farmers, the possibility of harvesting nature's own products has been important.

This was especially true during the 18th and 19th centuries, as the population increased. Norwegians always have felt closer to nature than citizens of other lands. In Norway, most wilderness is in the public domain; very little is privately owned. Those who want can harvest as much as they like, and that food can be a valuable contribution to the daily diet. We really don't know how lucky we are. In most countries, most land is privately owned, and few can hunt, fish or forage.

Today we speak of hunting and enjoying the great outdoors, and what we get from this can't be weighed solely in kilos or pounds. It is the experience of the whole, with its recreational value, which gives us better health and a positive outlook.

Gudbrandsdal is similar to the rest of the country as far as these activities are concerned. We have vast areas in the public domain, which we can use now, and which have been used for hundreds of years. We have wild reindeer, moose and deer, all kinds of wild birds, along with hares, and we have a vast choice of berries and plants which we aren't good enough at using. There are fish in the lakes, too. And there is enough control of catches, so that we are assured of continuity in the years to come.

But it's true that not all developments are positive. Society has taken its toll on these resources. There aren't as many animals or fish as before. Some animals have survived the

onslaught of society better than others and have increased. This includes deer, roedeer and moose. But if we look at wild birds, their number has declined. This is true for the larger varieties of grouse and the ptarmigan. We need to preserve what we have, and to be moderate in what we take from nature, especially now that there is an increasing interest in the outdoors, be it hunting or hiking.

We have to proceed carefully and make everything right, so that we can use and be proud of our natural resources, which are so sensitive to the smallest changes. Nature is our greatest resource. Since I am so fortunate to live in a district with vast areas of untouched nature, which includes fertile valleys, rushing rivers, old forests

and craggy mountains, I feel it is only natural to follow in the footsteps of my ancestors and use its gifts. This has become a lifestyle for me. Here I find plants which have been used for all sorts of things, from medicines for animals and people to food.

My nature is alongside a calm mountain lake on an August night fishing for trout or along a rushing river in June to try to catch a fish which is hiding behind a rock. It is a ski trip over a snowy mountain or a quick walk with a stop for coffee by the stone age settlement at Tesse, which may be as old as 4000 years. I still look for traces of the settlers under rocks, in natural caves and around the mountains here. Maybe I will find an arrowhead lost by a hunter 1000 years ago. All this is part of my concept of the value of life, and the expression, recreation, is not serious enough to describe it. Of course, it is recreation, but it is so much more.

Imagine sitting on a mountain in a storm, taking the time to watch and listen to its onslaughts, as it tries to banish life but never succeeds. Think about all the things around us with taste, ingredients we can harvest, so long as we harvest them correctly. Our ancestors have helped themselves to these resources and have found uses for them for thousands of years, and we can continue to do so.

Pride, respect and time. We need time for pride and respect, so that we don't accomplish what the storm has been trying to do.

Fish

Norway is a coastal country, and we are known for our seafood. Of 20 counties, only two are landlocked, Hedmark and Oppland, both of which are part of the Olympic region.

But they have fish, too, of the freshwater variety, with their own special traditions which we must preserve and continue.

Being a cook in an inland region is no longer restrictive. With good communications and good suppliers, we get just as fresh fish and shellfish as people living in the cities along the coast.

During the last few years, Norway has become famous for its salmon, which is farmed along the coast. Everyone agrees that Norwegian farmed salmon is the best, and it has become a major export item. But the export of fish is not a new phenomenon. Dried fish and dried saltfish have been exported from Norway to southern Europe for a thousand years, something we might forget in our enthusiasm about rising salmon exports.

As a cook in a typical inland district, I like to serve locally caught fresh fish. Unfortunately, the supply is seasonal, so we have to enjoy the fish during those months when they are available.

Around here, fish usually means trout, preferably mountain trout, the best of all. Of course, there are many opinions regarding which lakes produce the best fish. Each of us has a favorite lake. That goes for me, too. It is really the special traditions surrounding every fishing trip which produce the best fish, but I have to admit that there are certain differences from one lake to another. The best fish is the one which is the hardest to get, or the one from the lake the longest distance away. To go fishing in a lake or river today is a pleasurable and at times exciting experience. And, as in days of old, it might result in a meal or two. The catch tastes best when cooked on the spot, but it is also a good feeling to serve one's own smoked, marinated or fermented trout.

Being a chef in an inland district, with all the choices today, of both fresh and saltwater fish, is a big responsibility. I like to work with local ingredients, of course, but I also enjoy supplementing with ingredients from over the mountain. Traditionally, it is a short way from Lom to western Norway, and Bergen was the main city of contact until lines of communication were build through eastern Norway in the early years of this century. For us in mountain settlements, trout always has been our main fish. Even though other types of fish are found in our waters, trout is still the principal one. Farther east, other freshwater fish, including pike, whitefish and perch, are available. Most of us appreciate a fishing trip, and most of us like to cook our fish outdoors - that's the proof of a successful trip and the best meal of all.

Salad with Sautéed Mountain Trout and Herbed Sour Cream

It's never good to make a recipe too complicated, and mountain trout is best when simply prepared. For a meal with friends, I always try to recreate a little of the fishing trip itself. Maybe we are changing our emphasis, concentrating more on simple food, but with more atmosphere. The atmosphere around a meal is just as important as the food, if it is well-prepared.

2 trout, 250-300 g (9-11 ounces) each
oil or clarified butter
salt and freshly ground white pepper

Dressing

3 tablespoons sour cream

1 tablespoon sugar
1 tablespoon white wine vinegar
1/2 tablespoon finely chopped fresh basil
1/2 tablespoon finely chopped fresh chives
2 tablespoons lightly salted trout roe

a selection of salad greens

Fillet the fish, remove the small side bones and pluck out the bones in the center of the fillet with a tweezers. Cut each fillet in two. Sauté in oil over high heat, about 1 minute per side. Season with salt and pepper. Combine sour cream, sugar, vinegar and herbs. Stir in the roe.

Wash the salad greens and arrange on a platter or individual plates. Top with the fish fillets. Spoon over the dressing. Serves 4. Other types of fish can be used in this dish.

Mountain Trout Packets

Preheat the oven to 200 °C (400 °F). Tear 4 sheets of aluminum foil. Arrange a small pile of birch twigs on each sheet. Sprinkle 4 individual trout with salt and place 2 teaspoons butter in each stomach cavity. Place on the twigs. Form a packet of foil around the fish, folding the ends over to seal. Bake 40 minutes.

Serve with butter sauce and boiled potatoes. Let the guests open their own packets.

Fish Cakes

Access and taste determine which fish we use: Pollack, cod, plaice, flounder or haddock. If you can get pike, it's an excellent fish for forcemeat.

> 500 g (18 ounces) boneless fish fillets, preferably pike
> 2 teaspoons salt
> 1 1/2 tablespoons flour
> freshly ground white pepper
> 1 egg
> 4 dl (1 3/4 cups) milk
> clarified butter or oil

Cut the fish into small pieces and place in a food processor with the salt and the flour. Process until smooth, but do not allow the machine to get hot. Season with pepper. Add the egg and the milk, a little at a time – the milk should be the same temperature as the fish. Make sure that all milk is absorbed before adding more.

Form cakes with a spoon. Dip the spoon into cold water before forming each cake. Fry in clarified butter or oil over low heat. The cakes will rise a little. If the heat is too high, they will deflate. Count on 4-5 minutes cooking time. Turn several times while cooking.

Serve with sour cream, lemon, boiled potatoes and a salad. Serves 4.

Pickled Grayling

Many freshwater fish are even more plentiful than trout, and we need to use them more. Whitefish is one of these, and in some places, marinated and smoked whitefish have become popular. It is even fermented. Unfortunately, it is not found in north Gudbrandsdal.

Another similar fish is grayling, which is very plentiful here. During one night's netfishing in the summer, it is possible to catch enough to provide a whole day of work processing the fish.

Other kinds of fish can be used in this dish, which is a lot like pickled herring.

> 1 kg (2 pounds) fish
> 50 g (1 3/4 ounces, 2 1/2 tablespoons) seasalt

Wash the fish, scale and remove the head and backbone. Arrange on a platter and sprinkle salt in, over and under the fish. Refrigerate 24 hours.

Brine

> 5 dl (2 cups) water
> 4 dl (1 2/3 cups) 7% vinegar
> 1 dl (scant 1/2 cup) sugar
> 10 white peppercorns
> 1 bunch dill crowns
> 2 bay leaves
> 2 onions, sliced

Combine all ingredients for the brine and bring to a boil. Cool, then add the onions. Brush the salt from the fish and cut into 2-3 cm (1") slices. Place in a jar, cover with brine and seal tightly. Refrigerate 3-4 days before serving.

Pickled grayling keeps for several months, when refrigerated.

Pike

Pike is best in forcemeat. If we travel abroad, we discover that pike is more expensive than most other fish, because it is such a good binder. Fish cakes are a national dish, one which is experiencing a renaissance today. Freshly made fish cakes can be served for dinner or in sandwiches. Most fish can be used in fish cakes.

Pike Cakes with Vegetable Fricassee

500 g (18 ounces) boneless pike fillets
2 teaspoons salt
2 eggs, separated
4 dl (1 2/3 cups) milk or cream
1 teaspoon freshly ground white pepper
clarified butter or oil

Cube the fish and place in a food processor with the salt. Process until smooth. Gradually add the egg yolks and the milk or cream. Transfer to a bowl. Beat the egg whites until stiff but not dry and fold into the fish mixture. Stir in the pepper.

Refrigerate 1 hour. Form into cakes with a spoon, flattening them a little. Fry in clarified butter or oil over low heat. The cakes will rise a little. If the heat is too high, they will deflate. Count on 4-5 minutes cooking time. Turn several times while cooking. Serves 4.

Vegetable Fricassee

3 dl (1 1/4 cups) fish stock or water
1 dl (1/2 cup) dry white wine
100 g (3 1/2 ounces, about 1 large)
  carrot, shredded
100 g (3 1/2 ounces, about 12 cm (5"))
  of a thick leek, shredded
100 g (3 1/2 ounces, about 1/2 small)
  celeriac, shredded
150 g (5 ounces, 1/2 cup) cold
  unsalted butter
salt
juice of 1 lemon
2 tablespoons chopped chives

Bring stock and wine to a boil. Add vegetables and simmer 4-5 minutes. Beat in the butter, a pat at a time. Season with salt and lemon juice. Spoon some of the vegetable mixture on each plate. Top with fish cakes. Sprinkle with chives. Serves 4.

Salmon and Ocean Trout

Few fish are as prized as the Norwegian salmon, both for sport fishing and on restaurant menus. Around 1820, the first British sports fishermen came to Norway and began to fish for salmon. Maybe they were the pioneers of tourism in Norway.

Eventually, more and more Britons came to Norway to experience our fantastic nature, either to fish, to climb mountains, or to explore the wilderness. Fishing for salmon has contributed to the income of many a farmer lucky enough to own a stretch of river. Those who run hotels or rent out rooms for the night also benefit from salmon fishing.

Interest in salmon fishing has never been more intense than today. More than 300,000 Norwegians try to catch this noble fish during the summer months, in 400 large and small rivers.

Most of the salmon we consume today is farmed. Everyone agrees that our own farmed salmon is the best. The last few years have brought developments which have made this great fish even better. Using tanks on land has produced optimal quality. Everyone loves salmon. Even though farmed salmon is the cheapest and easiest to obtain, there is nothing better than a wild salmon. I think salmon is best when it weighs 4-5 kilos (9-11 pounds).

Here are some general recipes.

Red Fish Stock

Salmon Stock

1 kg (2 1/4 pounds) salmon heads and bones
1/2 carrot
1 onion
1/4 celeriac
1 teaspoon white peppercorns
1 teaspoon salt
1 bay leaf
water

Remove the gills from the fish heads and rinse heads and bones free from blood. Coarsely chop the vegetables. Place everything in a large pot and add cold water to cover. Bring to a boil and simmer 30 minutes. Do not boil the bones longer or the stock will taste like glue.

Remove from the heat and let steep 30 minutes. Strain, discarding the bones and vegetables, then reduce over high heat until half the original amount remains.

The stock can be stored 3-4 days in the refrigerator. It also can be frozen.

Stock made from white fish, especially white flat fish can be cooked longer, up to two hours.

Basic Recipe for Butter Sauce

3 shallots, minced
2 dl (1 cup) dry white wine
2 dl (3/4 cup) fish stock
1 dl (1/2 cup) whipping cream
100 g (3 1/2 ounces, scant 1/2 cup) cold
   unsalted butter
salt and freshly ground white pepper

Combine shallots and wine in a saucepan and reduce until only about 1 tablespoon remains. Add stock and cream. Reduce to about 1 1/2 dl (2/3 cup)Strain, discarding the shallot. Beat in the butter in pats and season with salt and pepper. If reheating, do not allow to boil or the mixture will separate.

Salmon Forcemeat

1 kg (2 1/4 pounds) boneless,
   skinless salmon fillet
1 tablespoon salt
1 teaspoon white pepper
4 eggs
1 liter (quart) whipping cream

Cube the fish and place in a food processor with the salt and pepper. Process until smooth. Do not allow the motor to get too warm. Add the eggs, one at a time and pulse several times. Gradually add the cream, making sure that all cream is absorbed before adding more.

Marinated Trout - Marinated Salmon

It is hard to avoid marinated salmon. In the world of gastronomy, marinated salmon is in the same class as Russian caviar and foie gras. I marinate both trout and salmon, even other fish. It isn't even necessary to use dill, for other herbs are just as good.

Fish for marinating should not be too small, for the fillets should be of a decent size.

For each kilo (2 1/4 pounds) fish, you need

3/4 dl (1/3 cup) salt
3/4 dl (1/3 cup) sugar
about 20 white peppercorns, crushed
dill

Fillet and bone the fish. Dry the fillets well. Combine salt, sugar and pepper and rub into both sides of the fillets. Place several dill fronds in the bottom of a dish large enough to hold an entire fillet. Place one fillet on the dill, skin side down. Sprinkle with the salt mixture, then with chopped dill. Place the second fillet on top, skin side up.

Refrigerate 48 hours, turning several times during the marinating process.

Serve with mustard sauce (see recipe, page 91).

Juniper-Marinated Trout or Salmon

For each kilo (2 1/4 pounds) fish, you need

3/4 dl (1/3 cup) salt
3/4 dl (1/3 cup) sugar
20 white peppercorns, crushed
2 dl (3/4 cup) chopped juniper berries

Fillet and bone the fish. Dry the fillets well. Combine salt, sugar and pepper and rub into both sides of the fillets. Sprinkle some of the juniper berries in the bottom of a dish large enough to hold an entire fillet. Place one fillet on the juniper, skin side down. Sprinkle with juniper berries. Place the second fillet on top, skin side up. Refrigerate 48 hours, turning several times during the marinating process.

Serve with mustard sauce.

Mustard Sauce

3 tablespoons Dijon-style mustard (do not use "hot dog" mustard)
1 tablespoon sugar
1/2 tablespoon vinegar
salt and finely crushed white peppercorns
3 tablespoons oil
finely chopped dill

Beat together until emulsified.

Juniper-Marinated Salmon with Herbed Cream Sauce

Herbed Cream Sauce

3 dl (1 1/4 cups) fish stock
1 dl (1/2 cup) white wine
2 dl (3/4 cup) whipping cream
2 tablespoons finely chopped celeriac
2 tablespoons finely chopped carrot
1 tablespoon finely chopped chives
1 tablespoon finely chopped fresh thyme
50 g (2 ounces) fresh spinach leaves, shredded
salt

4 thin slices juniper-marinated salmon

Bring the stock, wine and cream to a boil and reduce to about 4 dl (1 2/3 cups) over high heat.

Add vegetables and simmer until tender. Add the fresh herbs and let steep 1-2 minutes. Fold in the spinach and season with salt.

Spoon the sauce and vegetables onto individual plates and top with the salmon slices made into rosettes. Serve immediately. Serves 4 as an appetizer.

Salmon in Bouillon

6 dl (2 1/2 cups) fish stock
juice of 1 lemon
6-7 fresh mint leaves
1 teaspoon salt
6-7 fresh spinach leaves
1 scallion, shredded
10-12 snow peapods
2 tablespoons cold butter
4 thin slices raw salmon

Bring the stock to a boil. Add lemon, mint and salt. Blanch the vegetables about 30 seconds, then plunge into cold water. Reheat the vegetables in the stock a couple of minutes. Season with more lemon juice, if necessary. Beat in the butter in pats.

Pour the soup into heated plates. Place a slice of salmon in each. Serve immediately. Serves 4.

Sour Cream Mousse with Salmon and Caviar

8 sheets (or 3 tablespoons powdered) gelatin
2 dl (3/4 cup) white wine
8 dl (3 1/3 cups) 35% fat sour cream
500 g (18 ounces) poached or
    steamed salmon, cubed
4 tablespoons (1/4 cup) salmon caviar
salt and freshly ground pepper
2 tablespoons chopped parsley
2 tablespoons chopped chives

Dressing

1 dl (1/3 cup) whipping cream
1 dl (1/3 cup) white wine vinegar
1 tablespoon sugar
1 dl (1/3 cup) white wine
2 tablespoons salmon caviar

a selection of salad greens

Soak the gelatin sheets in cold water (or sprinkle the powdered gelatin over 1/2 dl (3 tablespoons) wine) to soften, about 5 minutes. Squeeze excess water from the gelatin sheets (disregard for powdered gelatin) and melt in 1/2 dl wine (melt the powdered gelatin as is). Combine sour cream, fish, caviar and the remaining wine. Carefully stir in the melted gelatin. Pour into a 1 1/2 liter (6 cup) loaf dish. Refrigerate until stiff, at least 3-4 hours. Dip the form in hot water a few seconds, then unmold and slice. Combine ingredients for the dressing. Arrange salad greens on individual plates. Top with a slice of mousse and a spoonful of dressing.

Smoked Salmon and Potatoes in Puff Pastry

2 sheets puff pastry
200 g (7 ounces) smoked salmon, in strips
200 g (7 ounces, about 1 large) blanched
  potato strips
1 tablespoon finely chopped fresh thyme
1 egg yolk

Preheat the oven to 180 °C (350 °F). Roll out the puff pastry sheets to twice original size. Combine salmon and potatoes and arrange on the pastry. Sprinkle with thyme. Brush the edge with egg yolk, fold over the dough and press together. Brush the top with egg yolk. Prick several times with a fork. Bake 15 minutes. Cut in diagonal slices and serve with white wine sauce flavored with fresh thyme.

Sea trout was perhaps the first farmed fish, but now it lives in the shadow of salmon. Many feel that fresh sea trout is just as good, but it has fewer uses. A fresh sea trout, weighing about 2 kilos (4 1/2 pounds) is the right size for baking in foil in the oven or for marinating. Just follow the directions for marinated salmon.

Potato Terrine with Marinated Trout and Cream Dressing

Cream Dressing

1 dl (1/3 cup) whipping cream
1/2 dl (3 tablespoons) white wine vinegar
1 tablespoon sugar
1 tablespoon finely chopped dill

Combine cream, vinegar and sugar, mixing well. Stir in the dill. Refrigerate 1 hour before using.

Potato Terrine

500 g (18 ounces, 2-3 large) potatoes
salt and white pepper
2 tablespoons chopped parsley
5 sheets (or 2 tablespoons powdered) gelatin
5 dl (2 cups) fish stock

Wash and peel the potatoes. Slice about 3 mm (1/8") thick. Blanch in lightly salted water, then plunge into cold water.

Preheat the oven to 130 °C (250 °F). Layer the potatoes with salt, pepper and parsley in a 1 1/2 liter (6 cup) porcelain terrine. Soak the gelatin in the fish stock about 5 minutes to soften. Heat to melt. Pour over the potatoes. Place a kitchen towel in the bottom of an oven tray (to keep the terrine from moving). Place the terrine on the towel. Bake 1 hour. Refrigerate at least 4 hours. Dip briefly in hot water, then unmold. Slice and serve with marinated trout and cream dressing.

Arctic Char

Arctic char is a new addition to our kitchens. Many places in Norway have access to fine mountain char, and its traditional uses are many.

Arctic char is not the same thing as mountain char. The former is a farmed fish, with dense rosy meat, much larger than its cousin. Most of the char farmers I know have philosophies similar to my own.

Arctic char is not so fat as farmed salmon and trout and therefore can be compared with wild fish.

Steamed Arctic Char on a Bed of Vegetables

3 potatoes
1 turnips
1 carrot
5 dl (2 cups) water
80 g (3 ounces) mushrooms
savoy cabbage or fresh spinach
salt
2 tablespoons chopped chives
400 g (14 ounces) skinless,
   boneless Arctic char

Peel and slice the potatoes, turnips and carrots. Bring the water to a boil and add the vegetables. Simmer until tender. Slice the mushrooms, shred the cabbage and add, along with half the chives. Season with salt.

Steam the fish over lightly salted water about 4 minutes. Divide the vegetables and their cooking liquid among 2-3 soup dishes. Top with the fish and sprinkle with the remaining chives. Serves 2–3.

Baked Ocean Trout with Creamed Onions and Mushrooms

This recipe is also good with salmon, ocean cat-fish, pollack and monkfish.

2 onions
1 tablespoon clarified butter
1 dl vermouth or white wine
3 dl (1 1/4 cups) whipping cream
150 g (5 ounces) fresh mushrooms
2 tablespoons chopped chives
2 tablespoons chopped parsley
salt and freshly ground white pepper
4 pieces, about 150 g (5 ounces)
    boneless fish fillets

Clean the onions and cut into small wedges. Sauté in clarified butter. Add the vermouth and reduce until almost all liquid has evaporated. Add the cream and simmer 5-6 minutes. Add the mushrooms and cook 2-3 minutes. Stir in the fresh herbs and season with salt and pepper.

Preheat the oven to 225 °C (425 °F). Place the fish on a greased baking sheet. Bake 5 minutes or until firm. The fish should be opaque, but it should not flake.

Serve with boiled potatoes. Serves 4.

Big Game

Moose

The need to find oneself as part of a greater cultural entity seems to be increasing.

For that reason, many feel there is something positive about hunting, not just the hunter. That's the way it is when many are forced to live away from nature. They need time to find that part of themselves.

I like to believe that most hunters have some of Jo Gjende's dream within themselves. He built a little cabin by Gjendeosen and lived there for most of his life. There he was free to philosophize about life and nature and to hunt reindeer and other game, which gave him a rich quality of life.

Even while he was alive, he was well-known. Now he has become a legend, Norway's best-known hunter.

The reindeer is our most important game animal from an historic viewpoint, but measured in number caught, moose wins.

In 1992, more than 30,000 moose were downed in Norwegian forests. That's a lot of meat. Here, as with everything else, it is important to prepare it right.

A great deal of moose meat is ground, and it can be used in recipes for ground beef. Almost as much ends up as stew meat.

Moose Stew

1 kg (2 1/4 pounds) stew meat,
   preferably from the shoulder or leg
butter
salt and white pepper
beef or game stock or water
1 kg (2 1/4 pounds) fresh mushrooms,
   preferably wild, quartered, if large
4 shallots, sliced
2 onions, in wedges
5 dl (2 cups) 35% fat sour cream
50 g (1 3/4 ounces) Gudbrandsdal
   cheese (Ski Queen)
cornstarch

Cut the meat into 3 cm (1 1/2") chunks. Brown in butter in a heavy skillet, then sprinkle with salt and pepper. Pour over stock or water to cover. Simmer 30 minutes. Add mushrooms, shallots and onions. Stir in the sour cream and cheese. Simmer 15 minutes more. Season and thicken with cornstarch stirred into a little cold water, if necessary. Serve with boiled potatoes or bread and a salad. Serves 6-8.

Note: Do not use low fat sour cream in this dish or it will curdle. If 35% fat sour cream is not available, use whipping cream or creme fraiche.

Moose Meatloaf with Lingonberry-Apple Sauce

This recipe makes use of ground moose meat and is a pleasant change from burgers and meatballs.

1 onion, minced
100 g (4 ounces) mushrooms, chopped
butter
salt and pepper
1 teaspoon thyme
1 kg (2 1/4 pounds) ground moose
2 tablespoons potato starch (or cornstarch)

Lingonberry-Apple Sauce

3 dl (1 1/4 cups) whipping cream
3 dl (1 1/4 cups) apple juice
2 dl (3/4 cup) diced apple
1 dl (1/3 cup) lingonberries
   (or chopped cranberries)
2 teaspoons thyme
salt
2 teaspoons cornstarch
2 teaspoons cold water

Preheat the oven to 200 °C (400 °F). Sauté onion and mushrooms in butter. Season with salt, pepper and thyme. Cool. In a bowl, combine ground moose with potato starch. Add the onion mixture and form into a loaf. Brown the loaf on all sides, then transfer to an oven pan. Insert a meat thermometer into the thickest part, and bake about 1 hour, until the internal temperature reaches 65 °C (150 °F). Let rest 10 minutes before slicing.

Bring the cream and apple juice to a boil. Simmer 10 minutes. Add diced apple, berries and thyme. Simmer 10 minutes more. Season with salt and thicken with cornstarch stirred into cold water. Serve with baked potatoes and autumn vegetables. Serves 6.

Salad with Smoked Moose and Raw Fries

Sometimes I like to try out new ideas with moose. I use the toughest part of the leg, eye of round, for this dish. It looks like a filet, but it is anything but tender.

2 liters (quarts) water
2 dl (3/4 cup) coarse salt
2 dl (3/4 cup) sugar
4-5 asp or willow twigs
1 moose eye of round
200 g (7 ounces) moose fat or suet

Bring water, salt and sugar to a boil. Remove the bark from the twigs and add. Cool. Pour the brine into a bucket. Add the meat, which should be completely covered with brine. Melt the fat and pour it over the brine to cover completely, so that no air gets into the brine. Refrigerate 1 week. Take it to the butcher for smoking.

Salad

1-2 heads Boston or cos lettuce
4-8 firm potatoes
clarified butter
salt and freshly ground white pepper
200 g (7 ounces) thinly sliced smoked moose
4 tablespoons (1/4 cup) sour cream

Rinse and dry the lettuce. Divide among 4 plates or arrange on a platter. Wash the potatoes, but do not peel. Cut into wedges and sauté in clarified butter. Season with salt and pepper. Arrange on the lettuce. Top with the smoked moose. Place a spoonful of sour cream on each portion and serve. Serves 4.

Reindeer

The domestication of reindeer has made this meat accessible to all. That's good, for it is probably the most Norwegian of all meats.

Great flocks of tame reindeer can be found all over the country. The Sami, the indigenous people of northern Norway, are the best-known reindeer herders. Reindeer have provided them with a living for centuries.

Many people I meet tell me they prefer the flavor of wild reindeer. I disagree. Tame reindeer and wild reindeer are the same animal, they live in the same areas and they eat the same foods. The difference is that wild reindeer follow their natural routes over the terrain, while tame reindeer are led by herders. The natural routes of those wild reindeer have been reduced by modern day life. Today, the quality of domesticated reindeer meat is consistent and better. I don't mean that wild reindeer should not be allow to roam as before. They are an important natural element of our country.

As far as meat quality is concerned, I prefer mature reindeer. The meat from fully-grown animals is the most flavorful and versatile. The way business is today, animals are slaughtered too young. Reindeer veal requires different treatment from the meat of mature animals.

Reindeer Soup with Small Mushroom Turnovers

Mushroom Turnovers

300 g (10 ounces) fresh mushrooms, cubed
2 tablespoons butter or oil
3 dl (1 1/4 cups) 35% fat sour cream
salt and white pepper
3 sheets puff pastry
3 tablespoons chopped chives
1 egg yolk

1 liter (quart) rich reindeer stock (see recipe for stock, page 36)
2 carrots, sliced
2 parsley roots, sliced
2 dl (3/4 cup) lingonberries
1 dl (1/3 cup) apple juice
salt
200 g (7 ounces) spinach, shredded

Make the tarts first. It is always difficult to recommend which mushrooms to use. I like cepes best, but any fresh mushrooms can be used. Do not used canned.

Preheat the oven to 175 °C (350 °F). Sauté the mushrooms in butter or oil. Add sour cream and reduce until thick. Season with salt and pepper. Cool slightly.

Roll out each puff pastry sheet until twice the original size. Divide each sheet in 2. Stir the chives into the cooled mushroom mixture. Divide the mixture among the 6 puff pastry sheets, spooning it onto one side of each sheet. Brush the edges with egg yolk, then fold the dough over the mushroom mixture, sealing the edges by pressing with a fork. Brush with egg yolk. Bake 15 minutes.

Bring the stock to a boil. Add carrots and parsley roots and cook until tender. Add lingonberries and apple juice. Season with salt, if necessary. Just before serving, add the spinach. Serve with the turnovers. Serves 6.

Note: Do not use low fat sour cream. If 35% fat sour cream is unavailable, use whipping cream or creme fraiche.

Marinated Reindeer with Gudbrandsdal Cheese

I prefer to use the filet (strip loin) on the top part of the saddle. Meat from the leg needs double the marinating time.

  1/2 kg (18 ounces) reindeer filet
  1 tablespoon sugar
  1 tablespoon salt
  coarsely ground white pepper
  4 tablespoons (1/4 cup) chopped
    juniper shoots
  1 carrot, shredded
  4 tablespoons (1/4 cup) chopped leek
  2 tablespoons shredded peppermint leaves

Trim the meat of all fat, membrane and gristle.

  Combine sugar, salt and pepper and sprinkle half on a dish. Arrange half the vegetables on the seasonings, then place the meat on the vegetables. Sprinkle with the remaining seasonings and vegetables. Place a light weight on the meat and refrigerate 48 hours.

  100 g (4 ounces) fresh mushrooms,
    preferably wild, sliced
  2 tablespoons butter
  salt and freshly ground pepper
  2 tablespoons raspberry vinegar

106

200 g (7 ounces) thinly sliced marinated
  reindeer
6-8 slices Gudbrandsdal cheese (Ski Queen)

Preheat the grill. Sauté the mushrooms in butter
and season with salt and pepper. Stir in the
vinegar. Transfer the mushrooms to a platter or
serving plate. Arrange the meat on the
mushrooms. Top with cheese. Grill about 30
seconds, until the cheese is soft. Server with
whole grain bread. Serves 4.

Reindeer Filet in a Sweet and Sour Cream Sauce

This is one of my favorite dishes, a permanent
fixture on the menu at Fossheim. I feel that reindeer is best in the fall, but we try to get quality
ingredients year-round.

900 g (2 pounds) reindeer strip loin,
  trimmed of all fat, membrane and gristle
butter
salt and freshly ground white pepper

Sauce

1 tablespoon unrefined sugar
3 tablespoons raspberry vinegar
6 dl (2 1/2 cups) stock
4 dl (1 2/3 cups) whipping cream
3 tablespoons cold butter
salt

Mushrooms and Spinach

300 g (10 ounces) spinach
500 g (1 pound) mushrooms
clarified butter or oil
salt and freshly ground pepper

Preheat the oven to 225 °C (425 °F). Brown the
filet on all sides in butter. Season with salt and
pepper. Place in the oven until the meat begins
to swell and firm up, about 5-8 minutes,
depending upon the thickness. Remove and let
rest on a cold tray 10 minutes. Just before serving, return to the oven for 2-4 minutes. Let the
meat rest a few minutes before slicing.
  For the sauce, melt the sugar carefully, then
add the vinegar and simmer a few seconds before
adding stock and cream. Reduce over high heat
until 5-6 dl (2-2 1/4 cups) remain. Beat in the
butter in pats. Season with salt, if necessary.
  Clean the spinach carefully. Remove the
stalks. Wild mushrooms are best, but domestic
will do. Clean the mushrooms well, but do not
wash. Slice. Sauté the mushrooms in clarified
butter and season with salt and pepper. After 2-3
minutes, add spinach and cook 2-3 minutes.
  Divide among 6 plates, top with meat slices
and nap with sauce. Served with scalloped potatoes. Serves 6.

Scalloped Potatoes

600 g (1 1/3 pounds, about 3 large) potatoes
1 onion, minced
3 dl (1 1/4 cups) sour cream
3 dl (1 1/4 cups) milk
salt and white pepper
grated nutmeg

Preheat the oven to 225 °C (425 °F). Cube the
potatoes and combine with the remaining ingredients in a large saucepan. Cook until tender.
Transfer to an ovenproof dish and bake until
golden, about 8-10 minutes. Serve from the
dish. Serves 6.

Roedeer

Roedeer is the most flavorful of all wild deer, but few other than hunters can get this meat.
If you are lucky enough the obtain a carcass, it can be divided much like lamb. The same holds true for its preparation. With such a special and hard-to-get meat, we have to be extra careful to prepare it properly.

Roedeer au Gratin

1 kg (2 1/4 pounds) boneless roedeer
   meat from the neck, arm or brisket
clarified butter or oil
salt and freshly ground white pepper
2 dl (3/4 cup) 35% fat sour cream
200 g (7 ounces, 5 dl, 2 cups)
   grated Jarlsberg cheese ·
50 g (2 ounces, 1 dl, scant 1/2 cup)
   black currants
1 tablespoon fresh or 1/2 tablespoon
   dried thyme or oregano
2 onions, chopped

200 g (7 ounces, 5 dl, 2 cups)
   grated Jarlsberg cheese

Preheat the oven to 200 °C (400 °F). Cut the meat into small cubes or grind it once. Sauté in clarified butter or oil in a heavy skillet. Season with salt and pepper. Combine sour cream, the first amount of cheese, currants and herbs and stir into the meat. Pour into an ovenproof dish and sprinkle with the onion and the remaining cheese. Bake 35-40 minutes. Serve with bread and a salad. Serves 6.

Deer

Most deer meat can be prepared in much the same way as beef. Sauce and side dishes are important for a successful meal. With deer, one must consider the delicate taste, which should come through in the finished dish. Deer meat is difficult to obtain in much of Norway. Most deer are found in coastal areas, and the traditions surrounding deer-hunting, naturally, are the oldest there. As deer gradually have moved east, more and more people have discovered this wonderful meat.

Coarse Deer Sausages

2 kg (4 1/2 pounds) deer meat
250 g (9 ounces) pork fat
1 teaspoon white pepper
2 tablespoons juniper berries
1/2 dl (3 1/2 tablespoons) salt
75 g (2 1/2 ounces, 1 dl, scant 1/2 cup)
   potato starch
3-4 m (yards) pork sausage casings

Grind the meat and pork once, then add seasonings and potato starch. If the mixture is too thick, add a little water. Fill the sausage casings and tie at intervals. Simmer sausages 15-20 minutes. Do not allow the water to boil or the sausages with burst.

This recipe also can be used for dried sausages. Do not add the potato starch. Add instead 50 g (1 3/4 ounce, 4 tablespoons, 1/4 cup) sugar, 2 dl (3/4 cup) aquavit and other herbs, as desired. Hang the sausages to dry in a frostfree, airy room. They should not hang close together, nor should they be against the wall. After 6-10 weeks, they are ready.

Deer Chops with Sour Cherry Sauce

The most tender meat is on the back, which extends from the shoulder blades to the tail. The area toward the tail without ribs is the saddle, while against the ribs are the strip loin on top and the filet underneath. If you loosen the meat from the backbone and cut it as close to the bones as possible, you get 2 fine pieces which can be cooked whole or cut into chops.

    4 large or 8 small chops
    clarified butter or oil
    salt and freshly ground white pepper

Sauce

    4 dl (1 2/3 cups) fresh orange juice
    4 dl (1 2/3 cups) cleaned, pitted sour cherries
    50 g (3 tablespoons) cold unsalted butter
    salt
    1 tablespoon fresh sage
    2 tablespoons chopped parsley and/or basil

Preheat the oven to 225 °C (425 °F). Sauté the meat in clarified butter. Season with salt and pepper. Place in the oven until the meat begins to swell, but before the juices begin to run out, about 5 minutes, but the time will vary according to the thickness of the meat. Let the meat rest 10 minutes. Just before serving, return to the oven 2-4 minutes.

Reduce the orange juice until half the original amount remains. Add the cherries and simmer 3-4 minutes. Beat in butter in pats. Season with salt, if necessary. Stir in the herbs. Serve with potatoes au gratin. Serves 4.

Small Game

The best known small game are hare, ptarmigan and grouse. These make up most of the total catch. Other, less desirable birds are pigeon, duck, goose and thrush. There are other types in the different regions, but the number caught is negligible.

Traditional uses for these ingredients often are local. Some areas and families have better access to these animals, so they have more experience in preparing them. Many people may not have enjoyed a ptarmigan before, but this is an excellent source of meat, one which we should be proud to use.

As with most things, there are a few basics which we should know. One important one is how to make stock. Do not cook the stock too long or it will turn bitter.

Here is my recipe for game bird stock.

Game Bird Stock

necks, backbones, thighs of ptarmigan
  or other game birds
gizzard contents (optional)
2 carrots
2 onions
200 g (7 ounces, 1 medium) celeriac
butter
water
1 teaspoon salt
4-5 white peppercorns

Chop the bones into small pieces. Clean the vegetables (do not peel the onion) and dice. Brown in butter in a heavy pot. Add water to cover bones, etc by about 2 cm (1"). Bring to a boil, then skim. Add salt and pepper. Simmer 20-25 minutes, then strain.

This stock is a departure point for a good sauce.

Ptarmigan Prepared Over an Open Fire

All hunters enjoy tasting some of their catch on the spot. As with everything else, ptarmigan is best fresh. Somehow, it just doesn't taste the same after a stay in the freezer.

Many think that ptarmigan is tough and needs lengthy hanging, but that is not true. The breast toughens if it is overcooked, even with fresh young birds. But hanging does mature the flavor and makes the meat more tender. This is true for all wild birds.

These last few years, I have begun to steam birds, for I think it gives the best results. Cooking in a cast iron pot or over an open fire creates an atmosphere which is perfect for the hunter. This is a dish which should be eaten then and there as a tribute to nature and its bounty.

juniper twigs, stripped of bark
water
1 ptarmigan per person, flayed
  (use giblets in another dish)
birch twigs or branches with leaves

Place the juniper twigs in the bottom of a large pot. Add water to the level of the twigs and bring to a boil. Place the ptarmigan, backbone down, on the twigs. Cover with birch twigs, which will serve as a lid. Steam 10-12 minutes. Let the birds rest 2-3 minutes before serving.

Roast Ptarmigan Breast with Giblets, Potatoes, Mushrooms

There are several kinds of ptarmigan, but all can be prepared in much the same way. Just be careful about the cooking time for the smaller ones.

Sauce

6 dl (2 1/2 cups) stock
3 dl (1 1/4 cups) 35% fat sour cream
2 tablespoons vinegar flavored with
   gizzard contents (see recipe, page 117) or
   other flavored vinegar
1 dl (1/2 cup) sweet homemade wine
   or port wine
1 tablespoon cornstarch
1 tablespoon cold water
2 tablespoons cold unsalted butter
salt
2 dl (3/4 cup) lingonberries or
   chopped cranberries

4 ptarmigan
1 tablespoon butter, melted

Giblets, Potatoes and Mushrooms

4 potatoes, diced
chopped gizzards and thigh meat from
   the ptarmigan
clarified butter or oil
200 g (8 ounces) mushrooms, chopped
100 g (4 ounces, 1 small) onion, chopped
1 bunch parsley, chopped
salt and freshly ground white pepper

Bring the stock to a boil and add the sour cream, vinegar and wine. Reduce over high heat until about 6 dl (2 1/2 cups) remain. Stir the cornstarch into the water and add. Beat in the butter in pats and season with salt. Just before serving, add the berries.

Preheat the oven to 225 °C (425 °F). Flay the birds, reserving the gizzard contents. Remove the giblets and chop. Cut out the breasts and leave whole. Remove the meat from the rest of the carcass and chop.

Sauté the potatoes, chopped giblets and meat in clarified butter. Stir constantly, so the mixture does not burn. After 2-3 minutes, add mushrooms, onions and parsley. Season with salt and pepper and continue cooking about 2 minutes.

Place the breasts on a baking sheet and brush with melted butter. Roast 6-8 minutes. Cool slightly, then bone and return the breasts to the baking sheet. Just before serving, return to the oven 2-3 minutes.

Cut each breast in 2 and serve with the giblets, potatoes and mushrooms. Nap with the sauce and serve broccoli alongside.

Note: Do not use low fat sour cream or the sauce will separate. If 35% fat sour cream is unavailable, use whipping cream or creme fraiche.

Potted Hare

I don't think hunters use much imagination in their preparation of hare. I may be mistaken, but I think most hares end up roasted with cream and served with lingonberry compote for Sunday dinner.

Hare is really very versatile. It is much like other meat, in that the hind end is tender and meaty, while the front end is tough. These parts should be prepared and enjoyed separately.

5 dl (2 cups) water
salt
400 g (14 ounces) boneless
   hare meat from the neck and arm
1 carrot, coarsely chopped
1 onion, coarsely chopped

Bring the water to a boil, then add the remaining ingredients. Simmer, uncovered 1 1/2 hours. Remove the meat from the broth and cool.

Grind or shred the meat and mix with:

1 dl (scant 1/2 cup) whipping cream
1/2 dl (3 1/2 tablespoons) cognac or aquavit
150 g (5 ounces, 1/2 cup) soft unsalted butter
4 tablespoons (1/4 cup) whipping
   cream, whipped
salt and freshly ground white pepper
1 dl (scant 1/2 cup) lingonberries

Pour into individual molds or a loaf pan. Refrigerate at least 4 hours, until set. Dip quickly in hot water, then unmold and slice. Serve with red currant jelly and a salad.

Wood Pigeon with Mushrooms and Potatoes

I don't think pigeon is served in many Norwegian homes. I don't believe very many areas have any traditions regarding pigeons. But, interest for shooting pigeons is increasing. That's understandable, for it is a tasty bird.

Pigeon can be prepared in much the same way as ptarmigan, but it has less flavor and smaller legs. This dish is made with mushrooms and a light potato sauce, rather than cream. In that way, the true flavor of the meat is preserved.

    4 pigeons
    2 tablespoons melted butter

Mushroom and Potato Sauce

    400 g (14 ounces) fresh wild or
       domestic mushrooms
    4 medium potatoes
    6 dl (2 1/2 cups) water
    salt and freshly ground white pepper
    100 g (4 ounces) fresh spinach

Preheat the oven to 225 °C (425 °F). Flay the birds, reserving the giblets, and wash well. Place in an oven tray, brush with melted butter and roast 6-8 minutes. Cool. Bone out the breasts and return them to the oven tray. Just before serving reheat the breasts 2-3 minutes.

Clean and slice the mushrooms. Wash the potatoes, but do not peel. Slice thinly. Bring the water to a boil and add the mushrooms and potatoes. Season with salt and pepper and simmer until the potatoes are tender. The starch in the potatoes will thicken the liquid. Clean the spinach and add just before serving.

Slice the breast on the diagonal and serve with the sauce. Serves 4.

Thrush in a Light Beer, Apple and Red Currant Sauce

This is more of a curiosity. There's enough thrush around, but we have no tradition in preparing this bird. It may not be meaty, but it tastes good.

    8 thrush
    4 large, tart apples
    2 dl (3/4 cup) beer
    2 dl (3/4 cup) red currants
    2 tablespoons chopped parsley

Flay the birds and bone out the breasts. Cut the apples into cubes the size of the currants. Simmer the apples 1 minute in the beer. Add the breasts and let steep 2 minutes. Stir in the currants and heat. Arrange on small plates and sprinkle with parsley. Serve with bread.

Serves 4 as an appetizer.

Wood Grouse with Creamed Mushrooms

Grouse are scarce, even for cooks. That's why it is important to prepare it correctly, to preserve the fine flavor and tender meat.

It's a myth that an older grouse is tough. It's often the cooking which makes the meat tough. That won't happen if you prepare it this way.

1 wood grouse, about 4-4 1/2 kg (9 pounds)

Creamed Mushrooms

1 1/2 kg (3 pounds) fresh mushrooms
clarified butter or oil
8 dl (3 1/3 cups) whipping cream
thyme and juniper berries
salt and freshly ground white pepper

Preheat the oven to 200 °C (400 °F). Pluck the bird and remove the giblets. Wash well and truss with cotton string. Roast 10 minutes. Remove and cool. Lower the heat to 100 °C (210 °F).

Wrap the bird in a large terrycloth towel, then in 1-2 layers aluminum foil. Bake 1 hour. Remove from the oven and lower the heat to 60 °C (140 °F). After the oven has reached that temperature, return the bird to the oven and bake 1/2-1 hour.

Clean and slice the mushrooms. Sauté in clarified butter or oil. Add cream and herbs. Simmer 8-10 minutes. Season with salt and pepper.

To serve, unwrap the grouse, cut out the breasts and slice. Serve with creamed mushrooms, almond potatoes, broccoli and lingonberry compote or cranberry sauce. Serves 6-8.

Marinated Black Grouse Breast

Just like its bigger relative, black grouse is tricky to catch, and often the hunter returns home with an empty sack. That's why it is important to use it well, to feed as many as possible. A bird which serves 2 as a main course serves 6 or 8 as an appetizer when marinated.

breast section of 1 black grouse
3 tablespoons seasalt
3 tablespoons sugar
4 tablespoons (1/4 cup) crushed
   juniper berries
1 tablespoon chopped fresh thyme
2 tablespoons shredded black currant leaves
1 dl (scant 1/2 cup) apple juice

Carve out the breasts. Combine remaining ingredients except for the apple juice and sprinkle 1/3 in the bottom of a small tray. Place one breast on the seasonings. Sprinkle with half the remaining seasonings, then top with the other breast. Sprinkle with the rest of the seasonings.

Pour over the apple juice and place a small weight on the meat.

Marinate 72 hours, turning the meat after 36 hours.

Slice thinly on the diagonal and serve on a salad dressed with herbed sour cream thinned with a little red currant juice. Other game birds also can be marinated.

Black Grouse Tartar

thighs from 1 black grouse or other game bird
2 onions
2 apples
2 heads Boston or cos lettuce
6 egg yolks

Scrape the meat from the thighs with a dull knife. There should be no gristle. Form the meat into 6 small patties. Cut the onions and apples into cubes. Wash the lettuce and divide among 6 plates. Place the meat patties on the lettuce. Sprinkle with onion and apple. Serve the egg yolks in half shells alongside. Serve with whole grain bread, salt and pepper.

Serves 6 as an appetizer.

Vinegar Flavored with Gizzard Contents

Anyone who has worked with poultry knows that the gizzard sits in the breast cavity. In that gizzard, the bird brings its own seasonings into the kitchen. It is always intriguing to find out just what the bird has eaten. You should never discard the contents of the gizzard, for they are a valuable kitchen resource.

No one is better at selecting the best plants in the forest and on the mountains than ptarmigan and other wild birds. Make an vinegar from this to use in dressings, marinades or in sauce.

1 part gizzard contents
1 part white wine or apple cider vinegar

Place the gizzard contents in a jar and pour over the vinegar. Screw on the lid. After a few days, it is ready. Leave the gizzard contents in the jar until the vinegar is used up.

Steamed Black Grouse with Herbed Juices and Vegetables

1 black grouse

Stock

neck, back and wing bones from the bird
1 carrot
1 onion
1 small leek
5-6 white peppercorns
6-8 juniper berries, crushed
1 tablespoon butter
water
salt

Side dishes

3 carrots
1 celeriac
3 parsley roots
2 large leeks
2 branches thyme (about 1 tablespoon fresh)
almond potatoes

Flay the bird and remove the giblets. Rinse and dry well. Cut out the breast section with a poultry shears. Start with the wings and cut down toward the point of the breast for one large piece with both breast filets attached. Use the thighs for another dish.

Chop the neck, back and wing bones into small pieces. Make stock according to the directions on page 110.

Place the breast in a pot on a rack, preferably one made from barkless birch twigs. Add water to the level of the rack. Cover and steam 15-20 minutes. Remove from the pot and let rest 15 minutes. Return to the pot and steam 4-6 minutes more.

Clean the vegetables and cut the roots into chunks and the leek into thick slices. Simmer with the thyme in the stock.

Prepare the potatoes separately. Carve the breasts from the bones and slice. Arrange the vegetables on a serving platter and top with the meat. Pour a little stock over and serve the rest alongside.

Set the table with soup plates, fork, knife and spoon, so that all can enjoy the thyme-flavored juices.

A Cultural Evening at Husehaugen
The Purity of Nature's Kitchen

Food is good. The right meal can be a pleasant memory for a long time. Everything has to fit together – the ingredients, combined with atmosphere, history and culture. There is nothing to compare with good friends around a table and a meal based on tradition, handiwork and philosophy, prepared with respect both for ingredients and guests.

Food and its preparation have attained a much higher status in Norway over the past 10 years. And for those in the kitchen, there are enough new challenges to guarantee a continuous development.

Everyone has a dream. Most cooks dream of opening their own restaurant. My dream has been to create an atmosphere where people come and live with me and taste the dishes from my kitchen. After a while, I found that it was difficult to have my own restaurant, but I am almost there at Fossheim. In a way, my dream became reality when I bought my little farm, Husehaugen, from my uncle three years ago.

I grew up next to this little farm, so my roots are here. It was my idea to have a place where I could live and have guests. I wanted to delve into the traditions of our region.

At Husehaugen, Unni and I have tried to create the perfect atmosphere for the perfect meal. People can visit us and wander through my history, learn about building customs and traditions, and try to understand just how difficult it was to grow enough to feed a family on a small farm years ago. Throughout the evening, people get to sample my dishes, spiced with a few stories between courses and maybe a note or two from a fiddle.

My great-grandfather, Jo Bjørviken, moved here in 1905. He had a tenant contract on the lot, which was comprised of 4 1/4 acres of fields, a small barn for animals, a small hayloft, a small storehouse and a small cabin. There couldn't have been much room, for at one end of the little cabin lived an elderly couple, and my great-grandparents and all their children lived at the other end, during the first few years. And they had to provide a stipulated amount of provisions for the couple who lived in the other end of the house. This included wood, water, grain, sheep and goats.

Great-grandfather tended the farm, great-grandmother the house. A lot happened on that tiny patch of earth, just as it did on all the other small farms. Great-grandfather bought the farm in 1919, to be exact, on August 19, 1919, and it has passed down on my mother's side since that time.

A menu at Husehaugen is, of course, in the spirit of nature's own kitchen. That also includes local building traditions and Unni's hospitality. We combine handiwork with our ideas about food and put together a menu with many flavors.

Part of the menu is served in the old cabin, which was restored recently. The main course is served around a long table in our new log cabin. I would like to give you an example of what I mean by such a cultural menu, and my reasons for choosing those dishes.

My bonds to the local milieu, to the culture and customs of the region have shaped me as a cook. Nature's kitchen first came about through my desire to use as much as possible of nature's gifts. Since then, this thought process has become a philosophy of life, which I practice every day.

Norway has a cultural heritage worth preserving. It is very rich, and food traditions are an important part of it. Our food culture is no less worthy than that of other countries. We just don't know it very well. The Norwegian kitchen has all too often been portrayed as a poor French copy rather than one with its own identity and special features.

It is a great challenge to preserve our natural

milieu, so that Norway can continue to offer pure foodstuffs, from fish and game to the products of the earth. This is a worthy departure point as we approach an uncertain future. People are becoming more and more concerned that what they eat should be authentic, pure and healthy.

In the Norwegian kitchen, we need the best raw materials, so it is important for food producers, processors and chefs to work together. The professional kitchen is often a trendsetter for the private household, and it is important for chefs to be able to communicate with the farmers, the dairies and the butchers. We all want a good result.

The Norwegian kitchen should be known for its use of high quality ingredients. We want our vegetables cultivated according to defined standards, and we want our livestock to be content and well-treated. Products should be handled with care from field to table, and at all stops in between – that includes storage, packaging, preservation and use of additives.

It is important that food from my kitchen be honest, that it doesn't try to be something it isn't. The ideal aim for nature's kitchen is to have full control over everything which goes into a meal. This includes supervision of growing and production of ingredients. Small-scale agriculture is the best guarantee of a high standard. We know from other countries that large-scale agriculture is more inclined to take shortcuts, with help from the pharmaceutical industry and purveyors of chemical sprays. This does not conform with our demands for ethical livestock production, our desire to conserve nature, and our need to know what we are eating.

A festive evening at Husehaugen is an experience steeped in atmosphere. My goal has been to integrate information about tradition and modern food preparation into the whole. I want my guests to feel that they are a part of Norwegian culture, and to have a meal which they will remember.

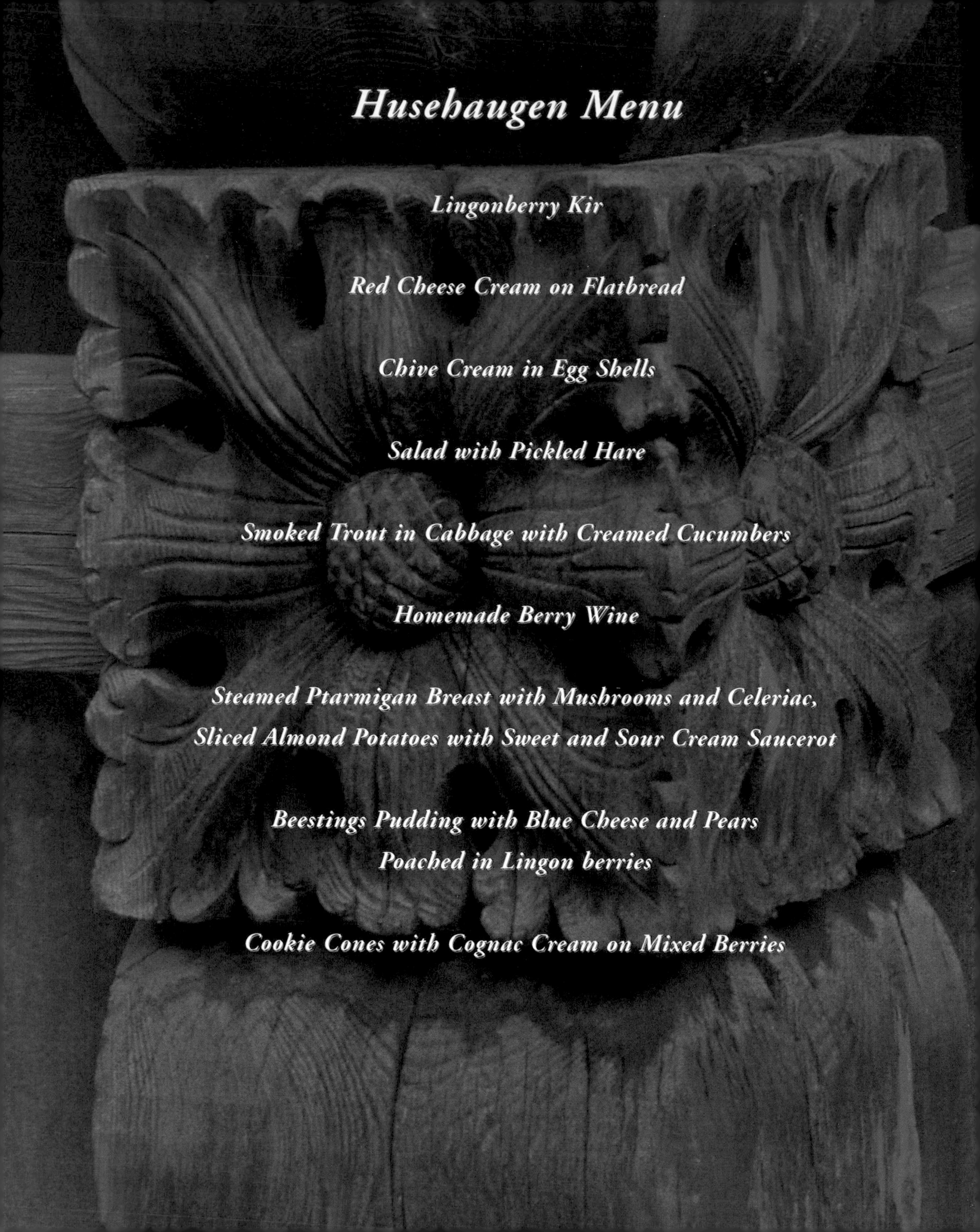

Husehaugen Menu

Lingonberry Kir

Red Cheese Cream on Flatbread

Chive Cream in Egg Shells

Salad with Pickled Hare

Smoked Trout in Cabbage with Creamed Cucumbers

Homemade Berry Wine

Steamed Ptarmigan Breast with Mushrooms and Celeriac,
Sliced Almond Potatoes with Sweet and Sour Cream Saucerot

Beestings Pudding with Blue Cheese and Pears
Poached in Lingon berries

Cookie Cones with Cognac Cream on Mixed Berries

Lingonberry Kir

It is always good to begin a meal with a cool drink to stimulate the appetite.

All Norwegians love lingonberries, and they can be used in so many ways.

100 g (3 1/2 ounces, 2 dl, 3/4 cup) lingonberries
2 tablespoons confectioner's sugar
1 bottle white wine

Purée the berries with the sugar and 1 dl (1/2 cup) wine in a blender. Sieve, so that the liquid is clear. Add remaining white wine.

Serve chilled in tall glasses. Serves 8.

Note: Cranberry juice can be substituted for the lingonberry purée. Sweeten to taste.

Welcome to my table
Red Cheese Cream on Flatbread

In our district, we often call Gudbrandsdal chee- se "red" cheese, for obvious reasons. I have dis- cussed the importance of this cheese earlier in this book, and it is only natural to serve it to my guests. (See recipe, page 28).

Chive Cream in Egg Shells

1 1/2 dl (2/3 cup) whipping cream
salt
2 small eggs
2 tablespoons chopped chives

Preheat the oven to 100 °C (210 °F). Bring the cream and a few grains of salt to a boil. Beat the eggs well. Combine with the boiling cream and stir in the chives. Divide it among 6 egg shell halves. Place them in an egg serving dish to keep stable and bake 10 minutes. Serve in egg cups. The cream should be a little soft. Serves 6.

Homemade Berry Wine

Homemade berry wine, such as a little glass of red currant wine, is a fine palate refreshener which also is a part of the natural kitchen. This dish marks the passage to new flavors and allows the guests to rest a little between courses.

Salad with Pickled Hare

We try to use only local products at
Husehaugen, and we try to be creative with
them.

This dish came about in that way, the result
of a hare in the hunting bag and the tradition of
using ingredients in the best possible way.

2 legs of hare
3 dl (1 1/4 cups) apple juice
3 dl (1 1/4 cups) juniper vinegar
1 bay leaf
1 onion, sliced
1 carrot, sliced
1 teaspoon juniper berries
a selection of salad greens

2 dl (3/4 cup) chokecherry
  dressing (see recipe, page 138)

Bone the legs. Bring apple juice, vinegar, bay
leaf, onion, carrot, salt and juniper berries to a
boil. Add the meat, cover and simmer over low
heat 30 minutes. Transfer the meat to a clean jar.
Bring the cooking liquid to a boil, pour over the
meat and seal tightly. Store in the refrigerator.

To serve, arrange salad greens on individual
plates and top with slices of the pickled hare.
Drizzle with chokecherry dressing. Serves 6.

Smoked Trout in Cabbage with Creamed Cucumbers

1 small wormwood leaf (optional)
1 dl (scant 1/2 cup) concentrated fish stock
2 dl (3/4 cup) whipping cream
freshly ground white pepper
500-600 g (1 1/3 pounds) warm
    smoked trout
100 g (3 1/2 ounces, 2 1/2 dl, 1 cup)
    chopped leek
6 large leaves celery cabbage
6 long leek strips

Rub the bottom of a saucepan with the wormwood leaf. Add stock, cream and a little pepper. Reduce to half the original amount. Mash 100 g (4 ounces) of the smoked trout and stir into the cream mixture with the leek. Blanch the cabbage leaves and leek strips 30 seconds, then plunge into cold water. Divide the cream mixture among the leaves. Roll up and tie with the leek strips. Serves 6.

Creamed Cucumbers

1/2 snake cucumber
water
1 wormwood leaf
3 dl (1 1/4 cups) concentrated fish stock
3 dl (1 1/4 cups) whipping cream
3 tablespoons chopped chives
salt

Peel the cucumber, divide in half lengthwise and remove the seeds. Slice and blanch about 10 seconds in boiling water, then plunge into cold water. Rub the bottom of a saucepan with the wormwood leaf. Add stock and cream and reduce to 3 dl (1 1/4 cups) over high heat.

Preheat the oven to 200 °C (400 °F). Heat the remaining trout with the cabbage rolls about 3-4 minutes. Stir the cucumbers and chives into the sauce and heat 2 minutes. Season with salt, if necessary.

Divide the creamed cucumbers among 6 dishes and top with a cabbage roll. Place pieces of trout all around. Serves 6.

Ptarmigan Husehaugen

Steamed Ptarmigan Breast with Mushrooms and Celeriac, Sliced Almond Potatoes and Sweet and Sour Cream Sauce

breasts of 3 large ptarmigan

200 g (7 ounces, 1 medium) celeriac,
   peeled and cubed
6 large almond potatoes or other
   waxy potatoes
300 g (10 ounces) mushrooms, sliced
clarified butter
salt and freshly ground white pepper

Sauce

  1 tablespoon unrefined sugar
  2-3 tablespoons vinegar made from
    gizzard contents (see recipe, page 117)
  3 dl (1 1/4 cups) ptarmigan stock
  3 dl (1 1/4 cups) 35% fat sour cream
  2 tablespoons cold unsalted butter
  salt
  2 teaspoons cornstarch
  2 teaspoons cold water

Steam the ptarmigan breasts, covered, on a rack over boiling water about 5-6 minutes. Remove from the pot and let rest 8-10 minutes. Carefully cut out the breast filets. Just before serving, return to the pot and steam, covered 2-3 minutes over lightly simmering water. Halve each filet lengthwise. One breast filet is enough per person with so many other dishes.

Blanch the celeriac cubes about 1 minute, then plunge into cold water. Wash the potatoes and boil in their skins until almost tender. Peel and slice. Heat clarified butter in a skillet, then add the celeriac cubes and the mushrooms. Sauté until golden. Season with salt and pepper. Add potatoes and sauté 2-3 minutes.

For the sauce, melt the sugar carefully in a large saucepan. Add the vinegar and let bubble a little. Add stock and sour cream and reduce over high heat to 4 dl (1 2/3 cups). Beat in the butter in pats. Stir the cornstarch into the water and add to thicken.

Divide the vegetables among 6 plates. Top with the ptarmigan breasts and nap with sauce. Garnish with fresh herbs, if desired. Serves 6.

Note: Do not use low fat sour cream in this dish. If 35% fat sour cream is unavailable, use whipping cream.

Pears Poached in Black Currants with Beestings Pudding

Beestings or raw milk comes from the second or third milking after a cow has calved. It is scarce, but anyone lucky enough to know a farmer might just get some.

Poached Pears

    5 dl (1 2/3 cups) water
    100 g (4 ounces, 2 1/2 dl, 1 cup)
      black currants, crushed
    150 g (5 ounces, 1 3/4 dl, 2/3 cup)
      unrefined sugar
    5 firm but ripe pears

Beestings Pudding

    4 dl (1 2/3 cups) beestings
    100 g (3 1/2 ounces) blue cheese

Bring water, berries and sugar to a boil. Peel and core the pears. Cut each into 6-8 wedges and add. Press a piece of baking parchment onto the pears. Simmer 20 minutes. Cool in the cooking liquid.

    Preheat the oven to 100 °C (210 °F). Pour the beestings into an ovenproof dish or into 4 individual ovenproof dishes. Crumble the blue cheese and sprinkle over the beestings. Place a towel in the bottom of an oven tray (to keep the dish(es) from moving). Place the dish(es) on the towel and add water to reach halfway up the sides. Bake 30-40 minutes, until set. Cool or serve lukewarm with the poached pears.

    Serves 4.

In my menus, I like to add blue cheese to the beestings and serve it as the cheese course.

Fortunately, it is more fashionable now to preserve old traditions. If there's a will, there's a way. At any rate, I get all the beestings I need during the calving season.

Cookie Cones with Cognac Cream on Mixed Berries

Cookie Cones (see recipe, page 66)

Caramel Threads

    100 g (4 ounces) sugar cubes

Mixed Berries

    5 dl (2 cups) water
    2 tablespoons honey
    6-8 mint leaves
    about 5 dl (2 cups) mixed berries,
       such as lingonberries, black currants,
       raspberries or others

Cognac Cream

    1 dl water
    100 g (1 1/4 dl, 1/2 cup) sugar
    1 vanilla bean, split lengthwise
    5 sheets (or 5 teaspoons powdered) gelatin
    5 dl (2 cups) whipping cream
    4 egg yolks
    1 dl (scant 1/2 cup) cognac

Prepare the cookie cones.

Melt the sugar in a wide, low pan. Cook until light brown. Cool slightly. Make sure that the sugar does not burn after it is taken off the burner. The pan is still hot, so stir carefully with a wooden spoon. When the sugar begins to make threads when the spoon is lifted, the temperature is correct. Place cookie cones on parchment paper and trail caramel over them, dripping it from the spoon. If it cools down, reheat.

Bring the water, honey and mint to a boil. Add thick skinned berries, such as lingonberries and currants, in the warm syrup. Cool, then add soft berries. Let the berries soak overnight.

For the cognac cream, bring the water, sugar and vanilla bean to a boil. Simmer 10 minutes, remove from the heat and steep 1 hour. Remove the vanilla bean and save for another time.

Soak the gelatin sheets in cold water (sprinkle the powdered gelatin over 2 tablespoons of the cream) to soften, about 5 minutes. Reheat the syrup. Whisk the egg yolks in a small bowl, then whisk in the syrup. Place the bowl in a saucepan filled with simmering water and beat until light and creamy. Squeeze excess water from the gelatin sheets (disregard for powdered gelatin) and melt. Stir the gelatin into the egg mixture. Whip the cream, add the cognac and fold into the egg mixture. Fill the cones with the cognac cream. Serve on top of the mixed berries.

At the end of the meal, we serve coffee, cake and traditional baked goods, such as wafers, simple wafers and rosettes (see recipes, pages 66 / 67).

A Culinary Meeting with Athletes

The location of the cradle of skiing is a matter of discussion. Telemark holds that honor, and that region fostered the great skier, Sondre Norheim.

Already before the 1994 Olympics, another Norwegian skier has become well-known, the Rødøy man, the ancient rock carving which is one of the Lillehammer Olympics pictograms. One thing is certain – we Norwegians like to think of ourselves as being born with skis on our feet. And since time immemorial, skis have been necessary for getting around in the winter. It is not so unusual that we regard skiing as our national sport.

Even though Lom is a neighbor of the mighty Jotunheimen mountain, it is not exactly a place people connect with winter sports. This is due to lack of precipitation. If we do get snow in the winter, it disappears fast. But we have mountains, and there's enough snow on them for year-round skiing. Jotenheimen always has been a legendary place. It is the home of the Norse gods, and in our own time, it offers all kinds of activity for people from the city, country and valley. More and more people flock to Jotunheimen. During the past few years, summer skiing at the Vetljuv glacier by Galdhøpiggen has been a big attraction. It is also a wonderful training ground for active alpine skiers. In fact, many national teams from around the world come to Lom to train during the summer.

The Sogne and Stryn mountains are popular gathering places for cross-country skiers. In this way, I have gotten to know skiers from around the world as well as our own, and they all appreciate a good meal during an active and demanding training period.

I have had the most enjoyable experiences with our own cross-country team, especially the men's team, which is a great group of guys, both as representatives of their sport and of our

country. I have been with them several times, at the world championships in Falun in 1993, and they have visited me at Husehaugen and sampled my food and heard my thoughts. Many of

132

them have even taken my cooking courses. All of this is especially gratifying. The Norwegian cross-country team represents something special in the Norwegian soul. That is why it is such a pleasure for me to have them as guests or to be with them when something good happens. But is mainly their own personalities and their team spirit which represent what they mean to us.

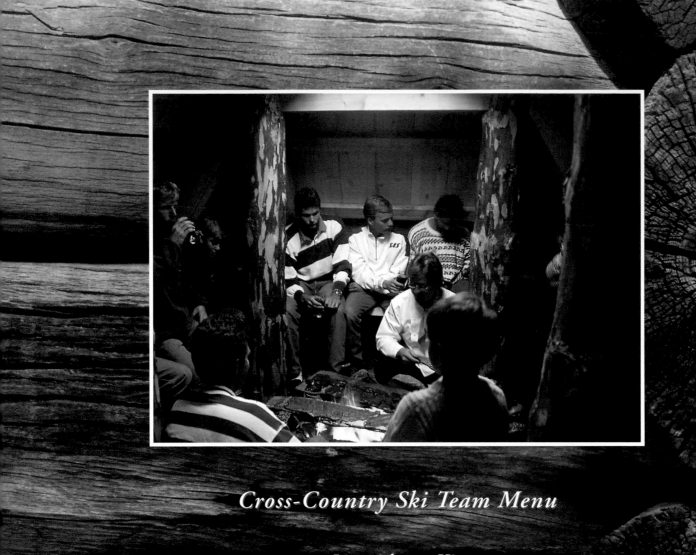

Cross-Country Ski Team Menu

Lingonberry Kir
Dried Moose Sausage on Flatbread
Salad with Sautéed Veal Sweetbreads and Chokecherry Dressing
Smoked Mountain Trout with Tiny New Potatoes in Mousseline Sauce
Reindeer Filet
Strawberry Salad with Warm Orange Cream

Smoked Mountain Trout with Tiny New Potatoes in Mousseline Sauce

Mousseline Sauce

5-6 shallots, sliced
1 liter (quart) salmon stock
3 dl (1 1/4 cups) dry vermouth
3 dl (1 1/4 cups) whipping cream
100 g (3 1/2 ounces, scant 1/2 cup)
   cold unsalted butter
6 egg yolks
1/2 teaspoon salt
juice of 1/2-1 lemon

Fish and Potatoes

300-400 g (10-14 ounces) tiny new potatoes
600 g (1 1/3 pounds) boneless smoked
   mountain trout fillet
100 g (4 ounces) snow peapods
butter

Combine shallots, stock, wine and cream in a saucepan. Reduce over high heat until 5-6 dl (2-2 1/2 cups) remain. Strain, discarding the shallot. Beat in the butter in pats. In a separate bowl, whisk the egg yolks 2-3 minutes, so that they will absorb liquid easier. Place the bowl in a pan of simmering water. Gradually whisk in the concentrated stock mixture. Whisk constantly, until the sauce is thick and light. Season with salt and lemon juice.

Leave the sauce in the bowl over the simmering water, while the fish is being prepared, but do not let it to get too hot.

Wash the potatoes well. Boil in their jackets until tender. Preheat the oven to 180 °C (350 °F). Place the fish on an oven tray and heat 5 minutes. Cut the potatoes in half and divide them among 6 plates. Top with the fish and nap with the sauce. Garnish with fresh herbs, such as chives or dill, if desired. Serves 6.

Salad with Sautéed Veal Sweetbreads and Chokecherry Dressing

1 liter (quart) water
1 carrot, coarsely chopped
1 onion, coarsely chopped
salt
6-7 white peppercorns
2 bay leaves
500 g (18 ounces) veal sweetbreads
clarified butter
freshly ground white pepper
a selection of salad greens

Chokecherry Dressing

1 part chokecherry vinegar
2 parts fresh orange juice

Bring the water to a boil and add vegetables and seasonings. Simmer the sweetbreads in the water about 40 minutes, until firm. Cool in the cooking liquid. Remove from the liquid and remove membrane and gristle. Slice and sauté in clarified butter in a hot pan until golden. Season with salt and pepper. Serve on a bed of salad greens and drizzle with chokecherry dressing. Serves 5-6.

Reindeer Filet

Sauce

1 tablespoon unrefined sugar
3 tablespoons raspberry vinegar
6 dl (2 1/2 cups) raspberry vinegar
4 dl (1 2/3 cups) whipping cream
3 tablespoons cold unsalted butter
salt

300 g (10 ounces) fresh spinach
500 g (18 ounces) fresh mushrooms,
 preferably wild
clarified butte or oil
salt and freshly ground white pepper
900 g (2 pounds) reindeer strip loin

Carefully melt the sugar in a large saucepan. Add the vinegar and let bubble a little, then add stock and cream. Reduce over high heat to 5-6 dl (2-2 1/2 cups). Beat in the butter in pats and season with salt, if desired. Do not allow the sauce to boil, after the butter has been added, or it will separate.

Rinse the spinach and tear out the stalks. Clean the mushrooms but do not wash, then slice. Sauté the mushrooms in clarified butter, adding the spinach after 2-3 minutes. Season with salt and pepper, then cook 2-3 minutes more.

Preheat the oven to 225 °C (425 °F). Brown the meat in clarified butter in a hot pan. Season with salt and pepper. Roast until the meat swells and becomes firm, 5-8 minutes, according to the thickness of the meat. Let the meat rest on a cold tray about 10 minutes.

Just before serving, return the meat to the oven 2-4 minutes. Let rest 2 minutes before slicing. Divide the mushrooms and spinach among 6 plate. Top with the meat and nap with the sauce. There is no need to serve potatoes with this dish, since they were served with the fish.
Serves 6.

Strawberry Salad
with Warm Orange Cream

Strawberry Salad

5 dl (2 cups) water
2 tablespoons honey
1 tablespoon sugar

6-8 mint leaves
300 g (10 ounces) wild strawberries
   or 500 g (18 ounces) strawberries

Orange Cream

4 dl (1 2/3 cups) whipping cream
rind of 1 orange
2 tablespoons sugar
4 eggs

Bring water, honey and sugar to a boil. Stir in the mint. Cool. Clean and slice the berries and add to the syrup. Refrigerate 2-3 hours.

Preheat the oven to 100 °C (210 °F). Bring cream, orange rind and sugar to a boil. Whisk the eggs, then whisk the hot liquid into them. Pour into 6 individual soufflé dishes and bake 15 minutes, until set.

Serve immediately. Serve the strawberry salad on a flat plate or deep dish with the orange cream alongside. Serves 6.

Postscript

Cooking is more popular than ever, and so is the search for roots.

This book has been written with the hope that we will find a more homey atmosphere around the dining table and be more aware of tradition in preparing food. I also hope this book will be part of the debate on just how food in Norway will be in the future. Some recipes are simple, some more work, but all are firmly based on Norwegian traditions.

We have many good ingredients, some worthy of an entire book. I am not able to include everything, but I have chosen what I do best and hope to spread pleasure with it. I want this book to inspire more people to enjoy and appreciate the time spent around a table with their loved ones, for good food contributes to the quality of life.

Good luck.

Arne Brimi

Recipe Index

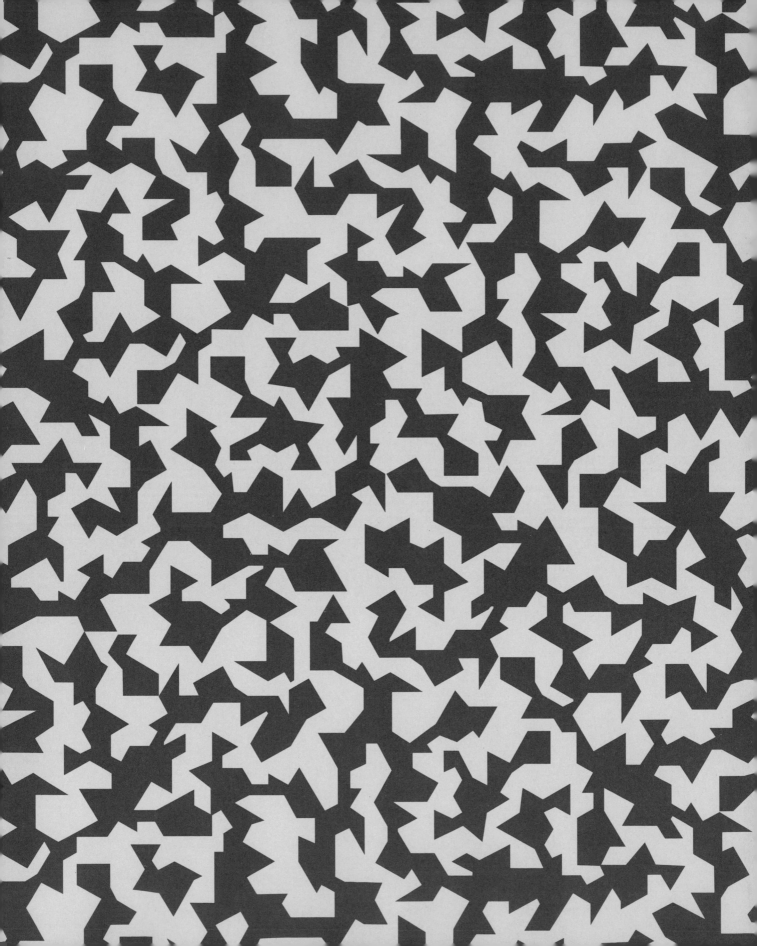